WHAT PEOPLE ARE SAYING

The Church Gathered is a vital part of God's plan and is extremely important. The Church Scattered is equally important. Dan Greer has done a great job in Church Scattered to help you develop an intentional plan that emphasizes the mission of the Church out in the communities in which we live. It will help you, who love the Church, make an increasingly greater impact for Christ in your community.

Dan Reiland
Executive Pastor, 12Stone Church

Dan gives our changing cultural conditions thorough and thoughtful analysis. As a Christian leader, we are all asking the same thing, "what next?" Our mission of the Great Commission is the same, but what will happen to our method? As the Church becomes scattered around the world, Church Scattered is worth the read.

Carey Nieuwhof
Bestselling Author of Didn't See It Coming and Founding Pastor, Connexus Church

Dan Greer understands the church and the marketplace and has put his finger on some natural tensions between the two. In Church Scattered Dan grapples with the role of Christians in the church—Church Gathered—and then in the marketplace—Church Scattered. Thankfully, when many observers are diminishing the value of the local church in the name of cultural relevance, Dan doesn't do that. Indeed, he maintains that the Church Gathered and the Church Scattered are "one church with the same mission." I commend this book to everyone as a primer on discovering and maximizing our calling as followers of Christ.

Mark DeMoss
DeMoss Partners

The landscape of the American Church is rapidly changing. In order to meet the needs of an ever-changing world, we don't need to figure out how to be more relevant, but rather to go back to the Scripture and look at the biblical blueprint for how to take the gospel to every tribe, tongue, and nation. Dan Greer has written a timely and thought provoking piece that will help pastors and church leaders equip the everyday believer to live on mission and see the gospel advance through a rapidly changing world."

Dr. Matt Carter
Pastor of Preaching and Vision, The Austin Stone Church

Church Scattered could not be a more timely call to action for the church to respond to the Great Commission. Dan Greer shares a clear, concise strategy of how people of faith can lead their clients, co-workers and neighbors through the COVID-19 crisis with faith, hope, innovation and vision right into the kingdom. The only question that remains is whether you are willing to answer the call.

Kathy Schrader
Judge, Gwinnett Superior Court of Georgia

Dan Greer has been a keen observer of church life for over 30 years. He has been on the executive leadership team of large churches as well as a church consultant. His observations on the directional focus of the church are spot on. In the coming years, the church will have to be much better at scattering in order to see its God-given potential realized—the church fully released where we live, work and play. Whether buildings remain relevant or not, this is the issue. Dan covers the ground masterfully. So many astute observations. A great read—you will be glad you took time to go through it!

Jim Sheppard
CEO & Principle Generis

Get ready to be powerfully convicted of our ambivalence as missionaries to our fallen world, which is right outside our door. If our goal is to enhance our careers to better our lives, we will live unfulfilled. If we live for our calling, our career is just one part of our strategy to reach the world for Christ. It is a means to a greater end. Church Scattered provides the roadmap for reaching and regaining three lost generations for Christ.

Laurie Tucker
Sr. Vice President of Corporate Marketing at FedEx (retired)

Disruption is the great initiator of change, and we are in the midst of one of the greatest disruptions in anyone's lifetime. As an excellent leader in the Church Gathered, and a strong enabler of the Church Scattered, Dan Greer shares lessons and insight that will challenge and encourage all of us. There is an enormous opportunity before us and God is on the move. The real challenge is how we respond to the opportunity right before us. Do we revert back to only what we know, or do we move forward into a new space that is very uncomfortable, but can transform our homes, work and neighborhoods?

Chris Cartrett
Executive Vice President, Aderant

One of the most refreshing books I've read in a long time. Challenging, practical, dynamic. A must read for Christians who feel side-lined, wounded and disillusioned by the institutional church. There is a place for people like us! And it's the tip of the spear!

Ed Gillentine
Managing Partner, Gillentine Group

Church Scattered gives us a blueprint for how to live as the church in the 21st century. Dan is clear on how "we are the church" and how we can live out our faith in our workplace, school and neighborhood. Church Scattered shows us how we can live out the Book of Acts now.

Phil Reynolds
Sr. Consulting Partner, The Ken Blanchard Companies

As Dan Greer shares in the Introduction "we have placed more value on the Church Gathered than we have placed on Christ and following him every day in the Church Scattered." Seldom in history has there been a more timely and compelling book for church leaders. If you truly desire to be the effective leader God made you to be in our day, RUN, don't walk to Church Scattered by Dan Greer.

Scott White
Executive Pastor, Redemption Church

Church Scattered is the modern-day version of Jeremiah 1:10. It is time to root up and to pull down in order to build and to plant. Dan Greer provides a roadmap for the changes we can implement to bring true kingdom principles into our daily life in order to positively impact the world.

Diane Kucala
Blueprint Leadership

This quote from the prologue sets the stage for what follows and provides sufficient reason to read further, "The current church model has failed to equip Christians to live out their calling in the other 95 percent of their lives ... " Dan has been on "both sides of the table" as a business leader and church leader. Readers will receive the benefit from his combined experience and wisdom.

Bryan Miller
Consultant

Dan's insights have helped me in a variety of ways over the years. The chapter on personal leadership from his recent work, Church Scattered, challenged me in fresh ways. Each of us is called to lead in our sphere of stewardship, regardless of our place in life. Saying "no" to good things in order to create "yes" margin for even greater things is a powerful, God-honoring concept I am more convicted of and committed to, thanks to Dan.

Dave Nelson
Chief Customer Officer, Armstrong Relocation

Never have we needed a more clarion, convictional voice on the diagnosis, prognosis and prescription of the current health of the church. This book will "disrupt" you personally, professionally and spiritually. It will challenge you to the core about what you have traditionally thought of as an effective church and your role within it. In Church Scattered, Dan gives us the framework and tools to change our approach to the way we relate to our church, our family, our career, our business, our neighbor… all for greater kingdom impact in the 21st century and beyond.

Bryson McQuiston
Home Instead Senior Care, Franchise Owner

Church Scattered—classic Dan Greer—really great content—insightful, practical, relevant, futuristic, disruptive, prophetic—clearly a high leverage message for individual followers of Christ and a playbook for churches which serve us!

C. Ashley Clayton
Vice President for Cooperative Program & Stewardship, SBC Executive Committee

In his life and ministry, Dan Greer is known for offering biblical, precise, practical, and often mind-blowing wisdom. His voice is one of the most valued and trusted in my home because his clarity and sober-mindedness have so regularly bolstered our faith and influenced our actions for the better. In Church Scattered, he does this yet again. This is a book that will sharpen, challenge, and inspire your faith, your church, your thinking, and your methodology. Dan's insight into disruption, the failings of the Church Gathered, and the hope for the Church Scattered is an essential message for the individual believer and institutions alike, especially as we strive to minister effectively during a pandemic that scatters us. Church leader, trust me: this is a "for such a time as this" message. Don't miss it.

Caroline Saunders
Ministry Leader and LifeWay Author

This book is cerebral, prolifically honest and direct about the challenges the church faces brought about by a continual and ever-changing worldview, and the economic and technological changes that impact our culture, and how leadership must align themselves spiritually and biblically to effectively lead the church in the future to come.

Kirk Sullivan
Founding member of Gospel Music Hall of Fame Group 4Him

If Bear Bryant only lectured his players on how to play football; only showed films from famous players on how to tackle, block, throw a spiral; and only drew "Xs and Os" on the chalkboard to explain assignments, then what do you think Bear's coaching record would have been? Instead, Coach Bryant had his boys practice in every condition possible, get dirty, and experience injuries and failure and taste success in preparation for the real games. Dan knows this and wants all of us followers of Christ to get out of the stands and into the ultimate game. And, this game is far more important than college football in the South; it's about eternity. If I don't care enough about my neighbor to get dirty and tackle the real issues in life, then I should stay in the stands. But what kind of love would that be?

Charles V. Welden, III
WeldenField Development, LLC

There are key moments in our lives where we realize we need to think differently to achieve a new outcome. While I wish we arrived at these moments of awareness on our own, they are usually triggered by a disruption that is imposed upon us. It seems that one of these moments of disruption has come to the church. In Church Scattered, Dan Greer compels us to think differently about what it means to be the church and guides us through the perspective shifts we need to make to see the church flourish today."

Jenni Catron
Author, Speaker and Leadership Consultant

This book revealed so much to me about my role as a disciple of Christ in the church during these trying times. If you are a Christian affiliated with a local church, this book will inspire you to rethink your own personal approach to the Great Commission. If we have the courage to listen to these words and then to let go of our failed "church mindset", we can create the opportunity for God to grow His people and the harvest will abound.

Kimberly B. Leousis
Senior Director of Institutional Research, University of Mobile

Early on in my ministry, I had the privilege of serving and being mentored by Dan Greer. The Church Scattered is not theoretical in his life; it is what he has lived and breathed for decades of faithful ministry. The Church Gathered and The Church Scattered is not an either-or approach, they are necessities and more important mandates for each believer. In his book, Dan has disrupted the traditions of many of our churches, and the result will be a church that thrives as it continues to deliver an unchanging message to an ever-changing world.

Matt Piland
XP Ministry/Leadership at Bethlehem Church

CHURCH
SCATTERED

CHRISTIANITY FOR THE 21ST CENTURY

DAN GREER

Church Scattered: Christianity for the 21st Century

Publisher: Grace Lake Publishing (May 19, 2020)
Language: English
ISBN-13: 9798986621517

Original Copyright © 2020 by Dan Greer
25899 Royalty Drive
Daphne, AL 36526

Editor: Stephanie Glines
Cover Design: Jason Garcia
Formatting and Layout: Jason Garcia

Printed in the United States of America.

CONTENTS

FOREWORD

I have recently caught myself wondering if I have been asking the wrong question as it relates to my 20-plus years of experience in vocational ministry. I've spent a couple of decades on leveraging most, if not all, of my resources on gathering people together, in one place, for worship and the teaching of God's Word. No matter the attendance at a particular address, on any given Sunday, there always seemed to be something missing. It's almost as if the question: "How can I grow the overall attendance of my church?" was just a small piece of a much larger question.

This is when I was introduced to the concept of the Church Scattered by Dan Greer. Church Scattered is a prioritization of equipping leaders to live out the gospel in their homes, workplaces, and neighborhoods. While the Church Gathered is still a biblical mandate and of the utmost importance, the Church Scattered is a biblical mandate as well. For far too long we've invited fellow followers of Jesus to sit in the stands to watch us (professional clergy) do church. It's not working. We are losing generations with this approach. This book provides very practical solutions to leveraging every Christian who calls your church home in reaching people with the gospel.

Church Scattered reminds everyone of what Paul says to every believer in Romans 8:11.

"If the Spirit of him who raised Jesus from the dead dwells in you, he who raised Christ Jesus from the dead will also give life to your mortal bodies through his Spirit who dwells in you."

If I was preaching this verse, I'd say: "Let me say that again," before reading it again. I don't have the luxury of doing that, so I'd ask you to indulge me and reread this very powerful truth one more time. Go ahead. I'll wait on you.

Here's a question for you. Do you believe what you just read? Do you really trust, for those who are in Christ, that we have the same spirit that raised Christ from the dead dwelling in us? If your answer is "yes," then you need to trust that your people have more biblical responsibility than just handing out cups of coffee, holding open doors, and passing offering buckets. It's time to unleash the power of the Church Scattered. This book will be an invaluable resource to help you do just that.

Blake Stanley
Executive Pastor 3Circle Church
Church Scattered Partner

I was first introduced to Dan Greer after a discussion about viewing work as worship and how to help other Christians live out the gospel in all areas of their life. My heart was then thrilled not only with his vision of the Church Scattered but also with the manner in which God has used Dan in both the secular and the sacred. Dan is passionate about being effective for the glory of Christ. I doubt there is a person on the planet who knows both theological issues and corporate leadership to the depth and extent Dan Greer does. A conversation with Dan about any biblical or leadership practice always proves fruitful.

From the day I met Dan Greer, I have been able to articulate into words a stirring that God had put on my heart many years prior to help Christians see the privilege of being in fulltime ministry. Everyone who is a follower of Jesus is in fulltime ministry. It's not just for pastors, missionaries, and those employed by the staff of a church. If we want to reach the world for Christ, then we must understand that all of us are in fulltime ministry, and where you go from eight to five is just the missional environment that God has you in during that time. *Church Scattered* takes this truth and gives it flesh.

Church Scattered will give you the tools to understand that we are to make a profit to then make a difference and help you understand that work is worship. This book will push Christian values and responsibility into all the corners of life. *Church Scattered* will help leaders become corporate shepherds and help you see that your work desk, boardroom, and elevator in your building are all mission fields. The business world is more likely to reach those far from God than any pastor could do on a Sunday morning. The Church Scattered movement is the hope and future of the church and will help strengthen it and build it. What a platform to proclaim the gospel! This book will also help pastors best shepherd the men and women who leave Sunday morning to spend the majority of their week in the business community, kitchen tables, and neighborhoods.

Church Scattered will help Christians fight the tendency to live the American Dream and encourage them to give their lives to proclaiming the kingdom of God. I pray that God will leverage this book for the glory of Christ and encourage the church leaders and corporate leaders to work together by equipping Christians to live out the gospel in every area of their lives.

Noel Fenderson
Entrepreneur
Church Scattered Partner

Dan Greer became a boss and mentor to me twenty years ago. He was teaching and living the Church Scattered principles then, and he has now articulated them in this incredibly important book. When he approached me about being a part of a team to lead the Church Scattered movement, I felt immediately a deep calling to accept his invitation.

You see, as a local church pastor and leadership coach, I have felt the unmistakable shifting of the ground beneath me for years. The tectonic plates of culture, technology, and behavior patterns are rapidly converging to an explosion of disruption that will forever change the way we do things. I, like most leaders, initially approached this situational fluidity by changing the game-plan. Like a coach installing a new offensive scheme, I wrongly believed the future could be navigated with simple strategy tweaks. This book makes an overwhelmingly convincing argument that this disruption requires actually changing the game completely and will get you started on the path to do it.

Churches tend to spend the majority of their resources and energy on the Church Gathered by creating great weekend experiences while often failing to properly focus on all the possibilities the Church Scattered offers the rest of the week. Church Scattered challenges this dichotomy without minimizing the importance of the gathered church. Rather than simply pointing out the inadequacies of our current strategies, this book shines light on a path that is full of exciting opportunities for the Church and the kingdom. It will open the eyes of a generation of pastors and leaders to the potential of unleashing the disciples sitting in our buildings into their own God-given mission fields to live and share the gospel.

The 21st century will require more of the church than ever before. *Church Scattered* will help all of us confidently navigate it to the glory of our God.

Chris Bell
Lead Pastor 3Circle Church
Church Scattered Partner

Church Scattered: Christianity for the 21st Century
Introduction

The church is not the hope of the world. Christ is.

Your security and significance in this life are not your career, marriage, or children. Christ is.

We live in a time of human history when it seems the whole world exists in almost total chaos, and we wonder every day what will happen next. The coronavirus is just the latest global reminder that we are not in control and how quickly fear can spread faster than any disease. Then, we read the words of Jesus and find comfort for our troubled souls:

> Peace I leave with you; my peace I give to you. Not as the world gives do I give to you. Let not your hearts be troubled, neither let them be afraid. (John 14:27)

Believing this in my heart is one thing but living it out in the daily decisions of life is another. If I can trust Jesus Christ for eternity, why do I find it so difficult to trust him for today?

If the abundant life promised to us is full of love, joy, and peace, why do we struggle under so much anger, fear, and worry?

Why, if we as Christians have been adopted as sons and daughters of God, do we live like slaves?

Why am I often emotionally moved on Sunday only to realize that by the following Saturday nothing in my life has truly changed?

Regardless of how hard we have tried as church leaders, why do my colleagues and I find ourselves just as ineffective in our mission as the average church member?

Consider this answer to the proposed questions: *the current church model has failed to equip Christians to live out their calling in the other 95 percent of their lives at home, work, and in their neighborhoods.* Our equipping strategy primarily requires people to sit in a seat on a Sunday to listen and learn, rather than training them to study for themselves during the rest of the week so they can spiritually mature and become an effective disciple. We have placed more value on what you will hear me refer to throughout this book as the Church Gathered than we have placed on Christ and following him every day in the Church Scattered—so much so that we have reduced the church to a mere commodity in the marketplace of our culture. The best facilities, family programming, music, and special events are competitive advantages that drive attendance.

This Church Gathered, codependent model meets the needs of the institution because, in the church world, attendance equals success. It is also much easier for members like me to attend a men's conference than to actually be the servant-leader we're called to be in our home and family.

The Church Gathered model in many churches has lost its effectiveness. In fact, Chick-Fil-A has had more moral influence on America's pagan, post-Christian culture than any church or denomination. The tip of the spear in the 10/40 window (a term used to refer to the rectangular area of North Africa, the Middle East, and Asia) is no longer a missions agency, but mission-minded businesses Christian executives are starting in order to effectively plant new churches.

In short, everything has changed, and this can be scary. In my work with corporate executives of large companies, I have seen firsthand that their number one fear is disruption, or the permanent change of a market's dynamics. Consider how e-commerce has quickly destroyed the strategies of many brick and mortar companies to the degree that many no longer exist. In the face of disruption, incremental change and realignment will not work. The only solution is radical transformation.

When it comes to ministry, I would like you to consider that we are experiencing widespread disruption, and we must begin a radical transformation process. The first step to transformation is confronting the brutal truth: we are not reaching three entire generations effectively because we have not equipped and matured the other two generations before them. If the church was a for-profit organization and our bottom line was the number of disciples we've made, we would have filed for bankruptcy a long time ago.

A disciple's metric for success should be nothing less than prioritizing the Great Commandment and then obeying the Great Commission every single day. When we passionately love Christ with all of our heart and our neighbors as ourselves, then the commission becomes the strategy not the goal.

However, I believe the situation we find ourselves in today is not solely because of the church failures and the implications of the post-Christian culture. I am equally convinced that the Creator is spiritually disrupting his church and scattering it once again as he has done so many times before. He is creating new wine that will not work in the old wineskins of current church methodology.

The purpose of this book is to inspire and equip Christians to discover their calling in life and release them to leverage every relationship for God's glory and their good. It is the merging of the sacred and secular priorities into a single life plan that is passionately committed to becoming a disciple and living on mission for Christ.

Just to be clear, the greatest responsibility for this change does not lie with the Church Gathered but with each individual Christian. You are not a pre-Reformation Catholic with no direct access to truth, but a Christian living in the 21st century with more biblical resources than at any time in human history.

We are to spend our lives in a passionate journey to know Christ and make him known. This requires the equipping and maturing of the individual believer so they can use every platform in their daily life to be the fragrance of God's grace.

The ultimate truth about discipleship is that the church is called to primarily support believers as they minister in their day-to-day lives, not just on Sundays. Only when we both properly align with our biblical responsibilities will we become the powerful force that can change the world for God's glory.

To the individual Christian who attends church on Sundays but isn't on staff: I am sorry if no one has ever told you that the biblical mandate for you personally fulfilling the Great Commission is no less than any professional clergy. We can no longer hide behind the segmentation of family, work, and faith because this biblical calling means that we are all 100 percent "in the ministry." Regardless of who signs our paychecks, we must integrate faith into every area of our lives and submit to Scripture as the ultimate authority for all priorities. We must also take the primary responsibility to own our spiritual growth and that of our families.

We are to be disciples who totally surrender to follow Christ, but we are also leaders and our most important client is ourselves. The greatest leadership challenge each of us will ever face is to lead the person we see in the mirror every morning. The hard truth is that we cannot pass on to others anything that we have not first lived out in our own lives.

My favorite leadership quote is from Thomas Watson, the former CEO of IBM: "Nothing so conclusively proves a man's ability to lead others as what he does from day to day to lead himself."[1]

Until we each accept this spiritual responsibility to lead in every area of our lives, we will never reach our potential for kingdom impact. As Christians, we must become effective leaders in our personal lives first; then, our leadership must extend into our homes; and, finally, it must extend into every platform of our public lives. It is simply not acceptable to succeed in one area and fail in all the others. One of the most important platforms we have is our family, and one of the most sacred places in life is the kitchen table. We each should make sure we have the spiritual, emotional, and physical margin we need to give them our best—not just our leftovers.

You can lead well at home and still be a great leader at work, with the ultimate goal of leading your team or organization from making a profit to making a difference. Meaningful relationships and bottom-line results are not mutually exclusive. In fact, if leadership is about influence, then the people who will have the greatest future impact on the kingdom will likely be in the marketplace and not in the pulpit. The front lines for the gospel have moved from the churches we attend to the companies where we work.

Think about it: the overwhelming majority of people in America today are not attending any church, but they are still going to work. If they don't see the reality of God in the integrity of our business plans and in the character of our leaders, they will probably never see it at all.

If you as a Christian leader are determined to be successful in every area of your life, then you will make the necessary commitments and adjustments needed to have the margin required for everything that is important.

Consider our current reality:

We take too much work home because we have not developed the leadership skills to get our work done in eight hours or we lack the character to say "no."

We live our personal lives with guilt and pain because we know that Christ and our families deserve better than what we are giving. Because we are not leading at home, we take our pain and guilt from home back to work and the cycle of failure continues.

We move from worry to anxiety to depression and eventually to burnout. We lose hope that our future will ever be any better than our present.

We lie to ourselves with self-talk that says, "Someday this will all slow down, and then I will make the changes I need to make." (Remember the accepted definition of insanity is continuing to do the same thing over and over again while expecting different results.)

This is not the abundant life Jesus spoke about. We must have the courage to stop living out the script that someone else has written for our lives and let God help us write our own. As Francis Chan says, "Our greatest fear should not be of failure but of succeeding at things in life that don't really matter."[2] If we don't set the priorities for our lives, someone else will gladly set them for us. To do that, we must know what our "yes" is in every area of our lives so we can say "no" with conviction to everything else.

We are living in very dark days, which means that the light of the gospel lived out in the power of the Holy Spirit is still the ultimate good news. As we seek to shepherd our families, our workplaces, and ourselves well, we must also reconsider our church methodology. After all, our message as the church is sacred, but our methods are not.

Most pastors know this and are prayerfully trying to do what is necessary to fulfill the Great Commission, but the concern over their church members resisting any serious change is a powerful force. However, they might be surprised to find more co-laborers than expected.

I was leading a meeting once, and some of these more drastic changes were being discussed with everyone in attendance. After about an hour of lively discussion, one of the senior adults came to the microphone. It is often assumed in a multi-generational church that the greatest resistance to change will come from the oldest members, so everyone (including me) braced for what was about to be said.

"I took my children to church, but now they have not attended in years," she said. "That also means that my sweet grandchildren, whom I love dearly, have never been to church either. What I have heard you say loud and clear is that as a church you want to prioritize reaching these next generations both here and around the world. Do whatever you have to do, and I will be your strongest supporter."

Meeting adjourned.

For Christians, "doing whatever we have to do" is more about total surrender than it is about being more disciplined. Our willingness to be under Christ's leadership is exactly what empowers us to lead others and ourselves.

Jesus Christ is not a commodity—he is the hope of the world. Welcome to Christianity for the 21st century.

Chapter One: Global Disruption

I don't think there has ever been a time in human history where change is occurring more rapidly than it is today. The global integration of the world's economies and the power of technology are two of the primary human factors that are driving this change. This is impacting our personal lives and families more than anywhere else; however, the Divine factor is even more significant. The Creator of the Universe is moving in even more dramatic ways to accomplish his sovereign will in the midst of this very broken world. He has waited patiently for his people to represent him well to the nations of the world, but we have been too busy serving idols that have taken his place of preeminence.

According to recent research, it is estimated that more than a billion people are living in the daily reality of desperately trying to find enough food to eat, water to drink, and a safe place to sleep, just to survive. They are trying to live on less than the equivalent of one American dollar per day. Another two billion people are also struggling to survive as they try to make ends meet with just two dollars per day. Multiple research organizations estimate that 26,000 children are dying daily from something preventable.

Richard Stearns, the recent president of World Vision, states the brutal facts: "There is much at stake. The world we live in is under siege, three billion are desperately poor, one billion hungry, millions are trafficked in human slavery, ten million children die needlessly each year, wars and conflicts are wreaking havoc, pandemic diseases are spreading, ethnic hatred is flaming, and terrorism is growing."[1]

Unfortunately, this is not "fake news" but the hard reality of the spiritual condition of the world today. As Christians banded together as the Church, we cannot simply look the other way and cross our fingers that it will all get better. There is little comfort in the thought that we did not cause all of this pain when we are doing so little to help reduce it, either.

David Platt serves as a modern-day prophet when he passionately declares, "I have been successful in my ignorance because they are powerless. Literally millions of them are dying in obscurity and I have enjoyed my affluence while pretending they don't exist."[2]

I have been a Christian for more than fifty years and grew up in one of the most crisis-filled decades in American history—the 1960s. The Cuban Missile Crisis almost led us into World War III and the daily threat of nuclear destruction was continually in the news. We witnessed an assassination of a president and the leader of the civil rights movement. African Americans were beaten, hung, and brutalized while many of our major cities were burning to the ground. The National Guard shot and killed four college students who were protesting one of the most hated wars of all time. The culture survived the sexual revolution and Woodstock, rocked with the Beatles, and topped off the decade by landing on the moon.

However, the pace of negative change I have been witnessing over the last twenty years is far more devastating than anything I experienced in the 1960s. In the midst of all the sheer insanity of that dark time, there was still a majority of people who embraced a Judeo-Christian ethic. That is no longer true today, and the significant increase in Christian persecution around the world, even in America, is a clear sign we have reached a tipping point.

In his popular book published in 1990, *The Frog in the Kettle,* George Barna shares an illustration involving a frog in a pot of water. If the water is extremely hot when the frog is placed in the kettle, the frog will immediately jump out. However, if you place the frog in room temperature water, it will gladly stay there, content with its surroundings. Here's the disturbing part: if you slowly increase the water temperature, the frog will not notice its changing environment. Eventually, by the time the water is boiling, it is too late for the frog to change its circumstances, and the end has come.[3]

Are we like the frog, failing to notice the ever-increasing temperatures around us and becoming complicit in our own destruction? If Christians serving through the church are the frog, and all the places where we live, work, and play are the kettle, the water is the culture. Believe me, it's getting extremely hot in here. One of the most important truths I want you to see in this illustration is that the hand turning up the temperature belongs to our heavenly Father.

Another key point that I don't want you to miss is this: the culture is not our enemy. The culture is simply the missional context in which we are called to live out the gospel each and every day. But, to reach the lost in our current culture, we must take a new approach. Remember, our message is sacred, but our methods are not.

For example, in our society today, if our marriages are no better than our non-believing co-workers and neighbors, then something is desperately wrong and must be changed now.

Barna sums it up well even in 1990: "It will be increasingly difficult to convince the unchurched that our faith is pertinent to the 21st century if the tools of our trade are from the last century."[4]

It is probably a good time for me to start unpacking some of my story. I have a unique background in that I have served about the same amount of time as a corporate leader and as a non-profit leader.

My time in corporate America included working for Burroughs, State Farm, and Reynolds Aluminum Company. I started my own leadership development company in 2007 and use speaking, training, and coaching to help leaders reach their potential. Two of my largest clients are Anthem and FedEx.

I have several years of seminary training and have had the privilege of serving in some great churches. My primary role was as an executive pastor in large churches, and I also had the great experience of helping start two progressive church plants in schools. I've benefited from a range of experience—from serving at Bellevue Baptist Church, a megachurch in Memphis, when it was averaging over 6,000 on Sundays, to seeing both small church plants grow beyond 1,000 in weekly attendance. Both of these experiences were rewarding and enlightening.

Despite the hours I've clocked in churches as an adult, I grew up during those crazy 60s not attending church at all. That's right, I'm one of those guys you did not want your daughter to date. You know, one of those hopeless, worst-case type people who no one thought would ever come to Christ. Incredibly, I began dating a beautiful young lady who happened to be a Christian. Church attendance became a small price to pay for the pleasure of her company and the enjoyment of her mother's cooking on Sundays.

I became a Christian at seventeen and for the first year I had to look in the Contents section of my Bible to find any book in it. Fortunately, that all changed in my early twenties when someone began to disciple me and teach me how to study the Bible for myself.

The reason my background is so important for you to understand is that at times in this book I will sound a lot like a corporate leader applying best practices. In the next few pages, I may sound like a church leader trying to figure out how to make disciples. Then to that point, my third voice is that of a committed disciple who wants you to passionately fall in love with Jesus Christ and enjoy living out his calling for your life as a Christian. If at some point while reading this book you have a hard time determining which role or voice is speaking, I will have accomplished one of my major objectives. My mission is to help you merge leadership and life, work and faith, personal and professional, and most importantly, the sacred and secular.

I desperately want you to see your work as a "white unto harvest" mission field and your kitchen table as one of the most sacred places in all of life. We have been told that we brought nothing into this world, and we can take nothing out. With that in mind, it's safe to say that "stuff" does not matter at all, but relationships will matter for all eternity.

We have been allowed to believe as Christians that being "all in" for Christ is reserved

My mission is to help you merge leadership and life, work and faith, personal and professional, and most importantly, the sacred and secular.

for the professionals. Our part is to show up and serve on Sunday (a very good thing!), but after we check that box, we move on with the rest of the week and on to all the other boxes. In this book, I am passionately going to do everything I can to inspire and equip you to put everything and everyone into one box.

The buildings you attend on Sunday mornings are not the holy places—you are. The God who created the universe actually lives within you and wants the two of you to do all of life together. What could be more incredible?

To set up this whole concept of disruption, let's look at some of the factors involved in experiencing or leading change.

One of the hindrances to change is that, bottom line, we as humans don't like change and would prefer to take a pass and stay where we are. We are like the frog, and the water still feels fine.

As individuals who need to change personal priorities or as leaders who are responsible for influencing change, we need to understand two critical approaches. Depending upon the willingness of the people in our care, we will either need to motivate change 1.) through pain of the present or 2.) by casting a better vision for the future.

If there is low or no commitment to change, then the pain of the present has to be greater than the fear of the future. We have to admit that what we are doing is not working and that we cannot stay where we are as the temperature increases.

The temperature of the water is not only increasing in our culture, but also in our personal lives. We are beyond stressed out and we seem to be failing with the people who matter most. Worse than that, we know that as Christians we have trusted Christ for eternity, but we have an extremely hard time walking by faith today. We have substituted busyness for blessedness. (Before we go any further, please hear my heart on this. The reason I am sharing some of these difficult realities is not to put you on a guilt trip but to remind you to embrace the truth you already know.)

The temperature of the water is clearly increasing in our churches. We have watched our churches decline in attendance in the midst of a growing pagan culture that hates almost everything we cherish. We are finally realizing that it is impossible to even parent in a postmodern culture if we have not taken the time to develop a personal biblical worldview as a reference for absolute truth.

We can't keep doing what we have been doing and expect different results. It's time to disrupt the status quo.

In his book *Disruption*, Mark Deymaz puts it this way: "Therefore, at a most critical moment in our nation's history, when demographic shifts are bringing change to America, most churches and the pastors who lead them are not framing the questions, shaping the narrative, or influencing the conversation beyond their own insulated audiences."[5]

Even as I urge you toward transformation, know that I am not writing this book to throw rocks and cast blame, but to admit my own failure to lead my family and myself well. As a church leader, it breaks my heart to know I prioritized coming to church over being the church for years. I don't make any claims to be some super spiritual giant. In fact, it is actually the opposite—I have failed a lot. Anyone can talk about the problem, but it takes someone who has experienced the brokenness of life to speak about solutions that really work.

I strongly commit to do everything I can to help you with all the practical, sustainable solutions you will need for the major challenges we face together. Though I'll mention big ideas and main points early in the book, I promise to come back to them later with helpful personal applications.

That brings me to the second, more effective way to lead change. Rather than increasing the pain of the present, we can cast a greater vision about a hopeful future that is far better than the negative reality of the present. This is the approach I am taking in this book because I assume if you are reading these words, you are hopeful and searching for a better way.

There has never been a more exciting time to be a Christian because we can leverage the disruptions of technology and globalization to have an even greater impact on the world for Christ. But, as exciting as this time is, it's also a time of great pain.

In the midst of these dark days, we can hold fast to two critical truths: 1.) Jesus promised to build his Church and the gates of hell would not be able to stop him. 2.) He began a good work in you as a Christian and will complete it and take you home to live with him forever.

CONTEXTUALIZATION

Let me shift into my Christian corporate leader role for a while to deal with one of the major disruptive truths in this book: the absolute biblical necessity of merging work and faith to represent God to the world through every context.

The best place to start understanding the concept of disruption and how it is fundamentally different from ongoing change is in the corporate world. Once we understand how disruption works, then we can apply those principles in all of the different contexts of our life.

"Therefore, at a most critical moment in our nation's history, when demographic shifts are bringing change to America, most churches and the pastors who lead them are not framing the questions, shaping the narrative, or influencing the conversation beyond their own insulated audiences."
- Mark Deymaz

This subject is extremely relevant to Christianity in the 21st century because in our culture, we spend the majority of our waking hours at work and we must leverage that time and opportunity for the gospel.

The book that helped me early on in my career more than any other was *Good to Great* by Jim Collins. In this book, he offers extensive research on why some companies sustain excellence over long periods of time while other once-successful companies eventually fail.

His opening sentence in the book is quite disruptive: "Good is the enemy of the great."[6]

When any one of us experiences a certain level of success that we consider "good," we become content with it, and eventually become complacent and resistant to change over time.

A leader who is already "good" in his or her field may develop a prideful attitude over time. He or she may believe they know what is best and will dictate to the market what it should want rather than humbly responding to what the customer actually needs.

Can this application be made to individuals, marriages, once-successful denominations, and churches? Absolutely.

Imagine the impact of "good" on marriages—if a husband begins taking his marriage for granted, one day he may wake up alone. He needs to make changes now before there are devastating consequences later. (I'll also be talking specifically about companies and change over the next few paragraphs but hang with me. It's all applicable wisdom for life outside the boardroom, and we'll connect the dots soon enough.)

When a company hires me to help them with leading change, it is extremely important to determine where they are in the change process. To help with this, I have discerned three types of change:

> *Developmental Change* is the normal, ongoing process in operational efficiencies and in some strategic initiatives. For example, developmental change is at work when companies find more effective ways to produce products at higher speeds and lower costs. (By the way, this kind of change is always necessary.)

> *Market Change* occurs when a major change is introduced, usually through technology or innovation, that permanently impacts at least one part of a company's value chain. (A value chain is simply the different

steps a company uses to produce and deliver goods or services. A typical value chain is research and development, operations and manufacturing, marketing, sales, customer service, and distribution channels.) A classic example of market change is Kodak, which had a record "good" year in 2000 but was unwilling to walk away from film and shift completely to digital. The company filed for bankruptcy in 2012. The only response to market change is realignment, which means not everything has to change (yet), but something significant must change.

Disruption Change is the most dramatic type of change, and it occurs when major changes, impacting multiple parts of a company's value chain, happen at an alarming pace and require total transformation within the entire organization in order for the organization to survive much less thrive. For example, if you were in the horse and buggy market in the early 1900s, life was "good." In 1918, only 8 percent of Americans owned a car. However, in just eleven short years the percentage of car ownership jumped to 80 percent. Goodbye, horse and buggy stores—welcome to full blown disruption. The auto market has settled into several decades of both developmental and market change with success for the most part. However, because of the introduction of new electric battery technology, self-driving cars, and ride sharing, this market is fast approaching another major disruption.

What does any of this have to do with Christianity and church in the 21st century? Everything, if you believe as I do that both our individual lives as Christians and the churches where we gather are in an undeniable period of radical disruption.

For example, as a church, when you live in Judeo-Christian America and all that comes with it, you can successfully use an attractional model to reach people. You can invite them to the Billy Graham crusade, spring revival, Vacation Bible School, and world-class children's programming, and they will likely come.

But the spiritual value chain has changed. Our culture is now postmodern, post-Christian, and heavily influenced by the often-toxic nature of the Internet that attacks biblical truth on every front. Now, an attractional model will no longer be effective. Because those who do not identify with any faith are not coming to hear the great new sermon series you are pushing on social media, you must radically transform to an intentionally relational approach at work and in your neighborhoods.

While the culture was dramatically moving from committed Berea to somewhere between pagan Corinth and pluralistic Athens, we were comfortably sitting in our institutional warm water. We've settled for "good" even though it's no longer effective, contenting ourselves with the thought that we still really want people to

Our culture is now postmodern, post-Christian, and heavily influenced by the often-toxic nature of the Internet that attacks biblical truth on every front.

come to Christ—as long as they come by using the same methods that worked for us in the past.

When we elevate our personal preferences above the biblical commissioning to make disciples, it has the same disappointing effect as a grumpy old man complaining about how much he misses rolls of film and going to Blockbuster. As General Eric Shinseki, the Chief of Staff of the U.S. Army, once said, "If you don't like change, you're going to like irrelevance even less."[7]

Leaders are not only seeing the effects of disruption, but they are seeing leadership itself change.

Let's go a little deeper into the work context to see how leadership theory has changed due to economic and cultural dynamics, and then we'll be able to apply it to other contexts and see what it has to do with Christianity in the 21st century.

In America over the last fifty years, we have moved from an agricultural age, to an industrial age, to the information age, and, now, in the last few years, to what many are calling the "idea age."

Simply put, in the agricultural and industrial periods people were paid primarily for what they did. In sharp contrast, during the current information and idea age, people are paid primarily for what they know and how well they think.

For the sake of simplicity, I am going to refer to the agricultural and industrial periods as the old model and the information and idea periods as the new model. If I were to describe leadership theory for the old model in one word, I would say, "positional," and for the new model, I would say "collaborative." The implications of this shift are huge.

In Stephen Covey's latest book, *The 8th Habit,* he states that in the 20th century positional model, the most valuable asset of any corporation was the equipment it had and the production process it managed. Under this model, the leaders at the top make all of the decisions, and the followers at every level simply carry out their instructions to the letter.

In sharp contrast is the new collaborative model advocated by Collins in *Good to Great.* The most valuable assets of the information and idea age will be the people within the organization and their knowledge and empowerment to get things done.

Does this new participative model mean that the leader has to surrender his or her role and all authority and responsibility are now totally delegated to others? Absolutely not. What it does mean is that the role of the leader has changed from the person with positional power to the person with relational influence. Today, if you have to tell someone you are the leader in charge, you probably are not. Add to this mix the power of technology and the rise of the ever-changing and highly competitive global economy, and you get the new realities for corporate leaders in the 21st century.

Let me use a simple illustration to demonstrate how leadership has shifted from the old model to the new:

> Imagine a leader operating under the old positional model (in which people were paid for what they did). He walks into the conference room at work, introduces a new program for the year, and gives each employee his or her individual assignment. He would follow up by asking, "Are there any questions?" This is a very directive style.
>
> Conversely, a leader operating under the new model of the information age (in which people are paid for what they know) walks into the conference room and says, "This is the new program we're considering for the year." He would follow up with, "What do you think?" and then engage everyone in the room to find the best collaborative solution.
>
> A leader operating under the new model of the idea age (in which people are paid for how well they think), walks into the room and says to the team, "What recommendations are you making for the year and why?"

As the world has transitioned from the older positional model to the new model, the leader's role has changed from the person with all the answers to the person who knows how to ask the right questions. Leaders must now make the shift to help transform and sustain the right organizational culture that places a priority on developing and empowering other people. Furthermore, many corporate leaders don't work only in an older American culture. They also have to contextualize their leadership to successfully lead multi-ethnic teams and communicate effectively with customers and suppliers from all over the world. Even more dramatically, the team members' role and level of personal responsibility have changed. If corporate leaders are going to be willing to delegate, the team members must be prepared to answer the questions "What do you think?" and "What are your recommendations and why?"

For this reason, a leader must ensure he or she has the right people—people who have the knowledge and the passion to make an organization the best in the industry and who will not settle for anything less.

In *Good to Great*, Collins says, "Those who build great companies understand that the ultimate throttle on growth for any great company is not markets, or technology, or competition, or products. It is one thing above all others: the ability to get and keep enough of the right people."[8]

The right people are what Collins calls "A players." As with the key leader, the issue is all about character. He goes on to say, "They will do everything within their power to build a great company, not because of what they will get for it, but because they simply cannot imagine settling for anything less. Their moral code requires building excellence for its own sake."[9]

Though I could talk so much more about leadership, I don't want you to miss the relevance of this concept of contextualization to your life and the resulting personal application.

In corporate language, context simply means that an organization fully understands its market, customers, capacity, and competitive advantage, so it can properly align all aspects of its strategy to be the most effective. Personally it means that you know at all times what your spiritual, emotional, and physical margins are in every area of your life. Margin is simply the gap between the demands on your life and your capacity to meet them.

Every day, we will have withdrawals from each of these areas, and it is our responsibility as leaders to make sure we are making the appropriate amount of deposits so we will have the capacity we need at all times.

Contextualization personally then becomes the supernatural wisdom and discernment to know what the demands are today and to make sure you have the capacity to meet them. If you don't have the capacity, then you have to reset new realistic expectations about what is a priority and what is not. For example: forget the laundry but get to the ballgame.

When we get into the realm of accomplishing the mission of God, we must again discern the context in which we are attempting to minister. In the purest sense, it is the attempt to present the gospel in a culturally relevant way.

Consider 1 Chronicles 12:32:

> *Of Issachar, men who had understanding of the times, to know what Israel ought to do, 200 chiefs, and all their kinsmen under their command.*

To make the point, Paul presented the truth one way in Berea and a different more culturally relevant way in Athens without compromising the truth in either situation. Jesus was the master of contextualization.

WORK-FAITH INTEGRATION

So, what do these changes in leadership culture in the 21st century have to do with the cultural changes that impact reaching three entire generations for Christ? Billy Graham foresaw this years ago and said, "One of the next great moves of God is going to be through the believers in the workplace."[10]

In the next several chapters, we are going to see how we as Christians, and the church as a whole, must radically change to contextually reach those who are without Christ. As the data shows us, the existing Church Gathered, Sunday morning focused model alone is overwhelmingly ineffective in making disciples, and thus the outcome is bleak. That is, until the church re-prioritizes all the work it has been called to do by embracing the Church Scattered model of discipleship in which all members and all unbelievers still live, work, and play together. This is not devaluing the Church Gathered at all—it's actually God's plan to save it.

In God's sovereignty, he has moved in corporate leadership theory at exactly the perfect time for Christians in the marketplace to relationally connect faith and work together. This is one of the major reasons why he is bringing radical disruption all over the world. He wants to be represented by a people living on mission seven days a week—not represented by a place we attend on Sunday morning.

Because ultimately all truth comes from God, some of the best leadership skills come directly from the Bible. The Book of Nehemiah is Harvard Business School-worthy, and, through the example of Jesus in the New Testament, it's clear that our Lord invented servant leadership.

Beyond dealing with disruption, the number one hot topic in corporate leadership is answering the question of how do existing Baby Boomer leaders (ages 55-73) learn how to effectively lead Generation X (ages 43-54), Millennials (ages 24-42) and Generation Z (age 23 and under) employees.

Sound familiar, church leaders? God is using corporate leaders to help figure out how to contextually lead three entire generations, which are exactly the same people we are trying to reach. Most of them are not regularly attending any church, but almost all of them are still going to work.

If we think like missionaries, we realize that these same three generations that value relational leadership over directive leadership would respond well to a relational approach from other Christians and a church that talks a lot about Jesus. Can you imagine the result if the church senior staff walked into a meeting with lay leaders and stopped trying to be Moses, handing down commands inscribed upon stone?

What if the conversations changed from, "How do we get more people to attend and serve?" to "What can we do to more effectively reach our city and change the world?" What if everyone in the room started asking questions like "What are the most challenging issues Christians are dealing with every day at home and at

"One of the next great moves of God is going to be through the believers in the workplace."
- Billy Graham

work?" Then, as they asked these kinds of questions, what if they collaborated to find practical ways to equip individuals to be more effective in fulfilling their calling in life?

These same generations that hate celebrity-driven, egotistical leaders at work tolerate them even less in the church. On the other hand, they are willing to work extremely hard for character-driven leaders whom they can trust and respect.

These three generations get a bad rap and are often considered lazy and shaky when it comes to what they believe and why. But lamenting the stereotype won't help when the greatest responsibility lies with the lack of leadership from the previous generations that created the global mess they are determined to clean up.

My generation is made up of men and women who were taken to church and emulated the hypocrisy displayed by our parents. We argued in the car on the way to church but held on tight to our smiles once we were inside. But the generations who have come after absolutely hate this—to the point they refuse to even be a part of this type of Christianity and church.

When I get the opportunity to coach these new generations, I understand completely why they distrust this type of behavior. The actual character qualities I address most often at these large corporations are honesty, humility, integrity, compassion, servanthood, caring, fairness, authenticity, and transparency. These generations are "all in" with profit-making, as long as the organization also prioritizes difference-making.

Because of this, it's been easy for me to steer their training toward things of faith. For example, because the hot topic of "mindfulness" is nothing more than a rebranded form of prayer, that opens the door to spiritual conversations. Additionally, because these generations are deeply interested in work-life balance, it's natural to introduce the role of faith in their total life plan.

Here's the truth: at a time when the cultural context is growing more difficult for the Church Gathered to be effective, there has never been a greater opportunity for the Church Scattered at work. Work moves up the priority list as something that must be valued if for no other reason than the tremendous amount of time we spend there. Bottom line, God wants you to take your faith to work. When it comes to work, however, there's another major disruptive issue that needs to be addressed: is work sacred or is it merely another secular activity we must leverage for good? Before we can cast a hopeful vision for a better future, we must deal with some of the hard truths of this important area.

In my opinion, the major problems that exist today in the work-faith conversation are more cultural than biblical. This is at the very essence of why it so hard to change, and it is why nothing short of disruption will work.

Any institution, even the church, will create systems and culture that ensure its long-term success. This is understandable and expected. However, our existing church institutional dynamics have created a dependency upon the church establishment that cannot be found in Scripture.

For many centuries, the man-made distinction between the professional clergy and the regular laity was almost solely for the benefit of the institution and not the people. I am not suggesting that our current church institutional dynamics are as harmful today among protestant evangelicals as they were prior to the Reformation, but some of the systemic issues are still with us today and are still very alarming. Even in modern churches, there are extreme examples of church leaders establishing themselves as the necessary dispensers of grace. When the church becomes the mediator between God and man instead of Jesus Christ, we have moved into a completely false gospel.

Thanks to the Reformation, the message of the gospel among evangelicals today has been restored to salvation by grace through faith in Christ alone and not through good works or church membership. However, the real biblical mistake is that the primary work of gospel proclamation is placed upon church organizational culture instead of upon individual Christians where they live, work, and play.

Someone said the first Reformation was about restoring the Word of God to the people, and the next Reformation should be about restoring the work of God to the people as well. It will take full-blown biblical disruption from the Father for this to happen. Why? Well, we are still having difficulty restoring the Word of God to the people. Most churches, though certainly not all, practice the belief that trained professionals are more effective dispensers of truth on Sundays than the ministry of the Holy Spirit working through personal Bible study during the week.

Here's the truth: at a time when the cultural context is growing more difficult for the Church Gathered to be effective, there has never been a greater opportunity for the Church Scattered at work.

I am not diminishing the importance of gifted preachers and teachers. I am, however, questioning a culture that measures success on disciple-making more by how many people show up to listen on Sunday than by how many live out their faith at home and work during the rest of the week.

As a church leader, I helped create this codependent culture in which attendance is the primary metric for success, both for the church and the Christian. The absolute greatest mistake was to assume that because someone was very active in church that automatically translated into spiritual maturity.

I do a significant amount of executive coaching of leaders in corporate life. One of the questions on my initial assessment of needs is "What role does faith play in your life?" I have been absolutely shocked and convicted at the number of Christians who have been active in church for decades and still do not know even the basic truths of the faith. It makes me think of Hebrews 5:12-14:

> For though by this time you ought to be teachers, you need someone to teach you again the basic principles of the oracles of God. You need milk, not solid food, for everyone who lives on milk is unskilled in the word of righteousness, since he is a child. But solid food is for the mature, for those who have their powers of discernment trained by constant practice to distinguish good from evil.

My personal experience has taught me that spiritual maturity does not really start in any Christian's life until they are getting more out of the Word on their own than through the ministry of others. There is simply no substitute for God speaking to you directly through your time alone with him. Consider these biblical truths:

> These things I have spoken to you while I am still with you. But the Helper, the Holy Spirit, whom the Father will send in my name, he will teach you all things and bring to your remembrance all that I have said to you. (John 14:25-26)

> But the anointing that you received from him abides in you, and you have no need that anyone should teach you. But as his anointing teaches you about everything, and is true, and is no lie—just as it has taught you, abide in him. (1 John 2:27)

No one can be effective in doing the work of God as a spouse, parent, neighbor, co-worker, friend, or small group leader unless he or she has understood and applied the truths of God's Word in their lives over time. If we are counting on hearing two or three sermons or lessons a month to adequately prepare us for the spiritual realities of living in pluralistic Athens in 2020, no wonder the work of God is suffering.

I don't wish to dismiss the calling of God upon certain people to serve in the biblical role of pastor or staff members, but I do desire to appropriately elevate the role of every Christian back to our biblical priority in accomplishing the work of God in the world.

This book is not primarily about right versus wrong, but the degree to which we are prioritizing some things over others. The Church Gathered and the powerful ministry it accomplishes for the kingdom is extremely important. On the other hand, if you look at just the amount of time we spend as the Church Gathered compared to the amount of time we spend as the Church Scattered, we must dramatically change our priorities.

The work of God has been given to all of us—not the select few. The calling of

God is not primarily about a vocation or location but a relationship. The highest expression of this relationship can be summed up in the term "Christian," which points to our position as adopted sons and daughters. The second most important term may be "disciple," a fully devoted follower of Christ and a servant leader of others.

Yes, the person who stands behind the pulpit has a sacred calling, but that calling is to be a Christian first and a disciple second. It is the exact same sacred calling that has been given to every person sitting in the pews who has trusted Christ for salvation.

Therefore, the expression of the work we do on a daily basis may be different, but it should not be any less sacred. As J.D. Greear, pastor and former president of the Southern Baptist Convention, says, "Answering the call of God is as pertinent for the business professional as it is for the pastor."[11] Actually today, the pastor who stands behind the pulpit will have far more challenges reaching lost people than the manager at work who interacts with hundreds of people every week.

The front lines of the gospel have moved from the churches we attend to the neighborhoods where we live and the places where we work. Divine disruption is behind this, and we can trust that God is doing a good thing.

THEOLOGY OF WORK

Pastor and author, John Stott, says, "Work is the expenditure of energy in the service of others, which brings fulfillment to the worker, benefit to the community, and glory to God."[12] In short, work can be—and should be—sacred. Because I wholeheartedly believe in the important and biblical foundation for this concept, I would like to offer you plenty of Scripture to make the biblical case that we should view our work as worship and as a vital avenue for God to accomplish his work in us and through us.

One critical text on this subject is in the first book of the Bible:

> Then God said, "Let us make man in our image, after our likeness. And let them have dominion over the fish of the sea and over the birds of the heavens and over the livestock and over all the earth and over every creeping thing that creeps on the earth." So God created man in his own image, in the image of God he created him; male and female he created them. And God blessed them. And God said to them, "Be fruitful and multiply and fill the earth and subdue it, and have dominion over the fish of the sea and over the birds of the heavens and over every living thing that moves on the earth." And God said, "Behold, I have given you every plant yielding seed that

The front lines of the gospel have moved from the churches we attend to the neighborhoods where we live and the places where we work.

In short, work can be—and should be—sacred.

In fact, the Hebrew root word for work is "avodah," which means "service," and its derivations are translated as both "work" and "worship."

is on the face of all the earth, and every tree with seed in its fruit. You shall have them for food. And to every beast of the earth and to every bird of the heavens and to everything that creeps on the earth, everything that has the breath of life, I have given every green plant for food." And it was so. And God saw everything that he had made, and behold it was very good. And there was evening and there was morning, the sixth day. Thus the heavens and the earth were finished, and all the host of them. And on the seventh day God finished his work that he had done, and he rested on the seventh day from all his work that he had done.
(Genesis 1:26-2:2)

The major takeaway in this text and the most important truth is that our great God worked and is still working today to leverage global disruption to reach more people for Christ. In fact, the Hebrew root word for work is "avodah," which means "service," and its derivations are translated as both "work" and "worship."

Secondly, this text clearly shows that man was given work to do for God. Because it came from God and is ultimately for his glory, it is most definitely sacred.

Of course, some of these verses describe the world prior to the Fall, so some of the dynamics have changed. It helps to divide the work of God into four major sections: Creation, Fall, Redemption, and Restoration. Prior to the Fall, work was clearly good and part of God's plan for his people. Now that we are fully into both the redemptive and restorative parts of God's plan, merging work and faith is vital.

Our own experiences testify that work is one of the primary means that God uses to both mature the Christian and then to use that witness to move others closer to Christ. We also see evidence throughout Scripture that work can be redeemed and used for the glory of God—more than I could possibly include in this book. (Side note: God is at Work by Ken Eldred is a deep dive on this subject and provides great insights.)

Jesus more than anyone else in history understood the importance of accomplishing his work so that our redemption could be provided and all of fallen creation restored. Notably, he is the most disruptive leader who has ever lived as well.

Consider these few verses:

And the scroll of the prophet Isaiah was given to him. He unrolled the scroll and found the place where it was written, "The Spirit of the Lord is upon me, because he has anointed me to proclaim good news to the poor. He has sent me to proclaim liberty to the captives and recovering of sight to the blind, to set at liberty those who are oppressed, to proclaim the year of the Lord's favor." (Luke 4:17-19)

For God did not send his Son into the world to condemn the world,
but in order that the world might be saved through him. (John 3:17)

Jesus said to them, "My food is to do the will of him who sent me
and to accomplish his work." (John 4:34)

I glorified you on earth, having accomplished the work that
you gave me to do. (John 17:4)

When Jesus had received the sour wine, he said, "It is finished,"
and he bowed his head and gave up his spirit. (John 19:30)

I do not ask that you take them out of the world, but that you keep them
from the evil one. They are not of the world, just as I am not of the world.
Sanctify them in the truth; your word is truth. As you sent me into the world,
so I have sent them into the world. (John 17:15-18)

When re-reading these familiar passages, we might think, "Well, after all, he was God in the flesh, so of course his work is sacred." But, on the other hand, we must not deny Jesus' humanity, and we must acknowledge that he went to work and shared his faith in every context of life as an example for us to follow. Here's a compelling question: when we become Christians, why doesn't God immediately take us to heaven? Re-read the last part of John 17 when Jesus essentially says to the Father, "Please don't take them out of the world but protect them and set them apart for the work I have given them to do." That work is nothing less than Jesus' work, representing the Father to the world in everything we do.

In addition to Jesus' example, there are also some clear admonitions in Scripture on the importance of working so you can provide for your family and help others.

Notice the connection in these passages between personal faith and sacred work:

But if anyone does not provide for his relatives, and especially
for members of his household, he has denied the faith and is worse
than an unbeliever. (1 Timothy 5:8)

For you yourselves know how you ought to imitate us, because we were not idle
when we were with you, nor did we eat anyone's bread without paying for it, but
with toil and labor we worked night and day, that we might not be a burden to
any of you. It was not because we do not have that right, but to give
you in ourselves an example to imitate. For even when we were with you, we
would give you this command: If anyone is not willing to work, let him not eat.
For we hear that some among you walk in idleness, not busy
at work, but busybodies. Now such persons we command and encourage

*in the Lord Jesus Christ to do their work quietly and to earn
their own living. (2 Thessalonians 3:7-12)*

*Let the thief no longer steal, but rather let him labor, doing honest work
with his own hands, so that he may have something to share with
anyone in need. (Ephesians 4:28)*

The Bible also clearly communicates the ways in which work is used to help with the character formation of a mature Christian and how God then uses that example to influence others toward Christ:

For where your treasure is, there will your heart be also. (Luke 12:34)

*No servant can serve two masters, for either he will hate the one and
love the other, or he will be devoted to the one and despise the other.
You cannot serve God and money. (Luke 16:13)*

*So, whether you eat or drink, or whatever you do, do all to the glory of God.
Give no offense to Jews or to Greeks or to the church of God, just as I try
to please everyone in everything I do, not seeking my own advantage,
but that of many, that they may be saved. (1 Corinthians 10:31-33)*

*And whatever you do, in word or deed, do everything in the name of the Lord
Jesus, giving thanks to God the Father through him. (Colossians 3:17)*

So, why is all this merging of work and faith so important? Why does it matter that we strive to be humble and committed to excellence at work even when our circumstances at work don't reward us? Why should we continue to do the right thing even if we are criticized, attacked, or even fired?

Scripture is clear on this as well:

*By this my Father is glorified, that you bear much fruit and so prove
to be my disciples. (John 15:8)*

*Now who is there to harm you if you are zealous for what is good? But even
if you should suffer for righteousness' sake, you will be blessed. Have no fear
of them, nor be troubled, but in your hearts honor Christ the Lord as holy,
always being prepared to make a defense to anyone who asks you for a
reason for the hope that is in you; yet do it with gentleness and
respect, having a good conscience, so that, when you are
slandered, those who revile our good behavior in Christ may be
put to shame. (1 Peter 3:13-16)*

The reason is simple but eternally profound. Eventually, because of your character, conduct, and conversations, people are going to know that you are a Christian. When others perpetually speak badly about other people behind their backs, by the grace of God, a Christian will not. When others take credit for work they did not do or cast blame on others for their failures, by the grace of God, a Christian will not.

Instead, the Christian who knows his or her work is sacred will strive to build up others, encouraging everyone from the CEO to the new intern. Eventually, through this ministry, people will start to see Jesus in that person. At some point in time, they will wonder, "What is the reason for the hope that lives in that man/woman?" When that conversation happens, the believer's life will be supernaturally changed forever. When that happens for you, work will immediately become worship, because the God who saved you is also now living in you to empower you to accomplish his will to redeem and restore. I can promise you that when we go to work instead of me, work becomes one of the most fulfilling facets of life.

This experience is what occurs when we are faithful to merge faith and work in order to make a difference in the place where we make a profit. In Christianity for the 21st century, what you do is no longer as important as why you do it.

I can say with absolute confidence that I have had more personal God moments working in the corporate world than I have ever had as an ordained minister. By the time I was in my mid-twenties, I was 100 percent in the ministry while working for a large corporation. To me, a "disciple" meant nothing less than a fully devoted follower of Christ and a servant leader of others. God had his hand in every area of my life and seemed to bless all that I was doing. New responsibilities and promotions came quickly, and I prayed fervently about the big decisions and the seemingly small ones that occurred every day at work.

My company had an executive leadership development program to equip high potential future leaders. In this program, they took a team of leaders out of their day-to-day roles for six months to travel and be trained to learn how to lead across the entire corporation.

The initial kickoff meeting was held in the corporate boardroom with all of the company's key executives in attendance. This was clearly my mission field, and, during the luncheon, I said to God, "It would really be cool if one day I could open a meeting in this room with prayer."

We traveled as a team and, of course, we shared a lot of meals together. My colleagues began to notice my simple practice of praying silently before every meal—especially the team leader who was not a Christian.

Eventually, because of your character, conduct, and conversations, people are going to know that you are a Christian.

Over those months, as people would ask about my story, there were many opportunities to have conversations about faith. At some meals, the team leader would ask me to pray before we ate our food.

Fast forward to the same boardroom where we were having our final celebration event with all the same important people. One of the executive vice presidents stood up to start the event, but our team leader interrupted him. He began to share with the group that it had become our practice as a team during some meals to have a blessing. He then asked me to lead that prayer.

I stood up to speak—because, after all, I had been doing this for years and why should this be any different? But five words in, it hit me, and I had to pause briefly to compose myself. The Father, in the middle of my prayer, took the time to remind me of my request six months earlier to be able to one day pray in that very boardroom. It was one of the most sacred moments of my life as we finished the prayer together and sat down.

After the meal, an executive, whom I had never met before but was a committed Christian, pulled me to the side and said, "I have no idea what just happened, but I have worked here for over thirty years and that is the first prayer I have ever heard in this building."

Maybe now more than any other time in history, the world needs mature Christian leaders to be "all in" by merging all of the secular and sacred areas to fulfill God's calling on their lives. I love this quote:

> The world needs men and women…
> Who cannot be bought,
> Whose word is their bond,
> Who put character above wealth,
> Who possess opinions and a will,
> Who are larger than their vocations,
> Who do not hesitate to take changes,
> Who will not lose their individuality in a crowd,
> Who will be as honest in small things as in great things,
> Who will make no compromise with wrong,
> Whose ambitions are not confined to their own selfish desires,
> Who will not say they do it because everybody else does it,
> Who are true to their friends,
> Who do not believe that shrewdness, cunning, and hard-headedness are the best qualities for success,
> Who are not ashamed or afraid to stand for the truth when it is unpopular,
> Who can say "no" with emphasis although all the rest of the world says "yes." – Author Unknown [13]

PRACTICAL APPLICATION

In every chapter, I will summarize the major disruptive truths presented and in the Appendix will offer practical ways to respond to them. This is my attempt to connect you with additional organizations and resources that will be worth your time to research and partner with moving forward.

DISRUPTIVE TRUTHS

God is leveraging global disruption to dramatically change the priorities for Christians and the church to accomplish his mission of redemption and restoration in the world.

We have allowed the institutional culture of the church to define our success more than Christians living out the gospel at home, work, and in their neighborhoods.

Every Christian is called to be a disciple and to leverage his or her work as part of God's sacred mission for his or her life.

Chapter Two: Cultural Disruption

The fallout from global disruption is radically changing our lives both personally and professionally. For all Christians, especially those who are married and parenting, all of this is extremely relevant to your life. We must develop a biblical worldview that safeguards us from overreacting every time the president blasts out a tweet.

I urge you to understand what is going on in today's believing culture in order to help families effectively navigate living the Christian life as a persecuted minority. Thankfully, we have been promised the grace we will need, and we can leverage this disruption for God's glory.

Chaos is going to be the new normal for our future, and we need to build the spiritual maturity into our lives that will help us spend our God-given time wisely.

Chaos is going to be the new normal for our future, and we need to build the spiritual maturity into our lives that will help us spend our God-given time wisely. Again, the culture is not our enemy, but an evolving arena where ministry takes place. We must place our relationship with our Father as the most important relationship we invest in daily—to be rooted in his ways rather than blown about by every wind of new teaching, as Ephesians 4:14 instructs.

In the final three chapters of this book, I am going to give you practical tools to ensure that you have the ability to gain margin in every area of your life. I have been practicing these disciplines for years and have witnessed them work in the lives of many others.

This newfound margin will need to be spent on the most important values, not just the urgent ones. Quite frankly, if you are married with children, that particular arena will likely be the one you will need to prioritize in order to affect positive change.

As a verse of great comfort says:

> Behold, the hour is coming, indeed it has come, when you will be scattered, each to his own home, and will leave me alone. Yet I am not alone, for the Father is with me. I have said these things to you, that in me you may have peace. In the world you will have tribulation. But take heart; I have overcome the world. (John 16:32-33)

I mentioned that when something is truly in disruption, a simple realignment or marginal change is not enough to bring about a solution. The only resolution for disruption is a radical transformation to what we believe and how we behave.

This degree of change is necessary in every aspect of our lives: personally, professionally, in our marriages, in our parenting, in our churches, and with our friends and neighbors.

When I was parenting, all of the monsters under the bed were fictitious, but, in our world today, they live on our devices and are very real.

Contextualization is another critical factor in understanding what has shifted and why. If we don't clearly understand the context, then we have no chance of offering a better alternative. As I mentioned before, this is not the 60s; it is actually much worse. Tim Keller points to one of the reasons why:

"Historically, even if you didn't really love God, it was culturally expected that you went to church and lived a decently moral life. But now if you go to church and try to live a moral life, especially if you stand for biblical values, you're labeled judgmental and closed-minded."[1]

I want to begin the discussion of contextualization as it relates to the corporate aspect of our lives because work is one of the most disrupted areas of our lives, and, therefore, in a significant way, is already impacting us all with mass amounts of stress. We spend most of our waking hours in the workplace, and, for too many Christians, this sadly has become the primary place where security and significance in life are found. Contextually, faith and family are listed low on the priority list many times because work issues are seemingly the most urgent and most important matters.

The other difficult reality of that dynamic is, as was the case for most of my life, we are better people and better leaders at work than we are at home. My employers got the best of what I had to offer every day, while my family had to settle for the leftovers.

I mentioned earlier that corporate America is desperately trying to figure out these last three generations who are showing up to work every day. Millennials have a passion for making a difference in the world, and they are not interested in making a profit just to give more money to the wealthy class.

A recurring biblical theme is that God is more concerned with the heart of a person rather than his or her outward appearance. This directly connects to the leadership priorities of character over competence. When we are training and coaching about integrity, humility, and honesty, we have migrated into the faith culture whether we realize it or not.

Tragically, the church has viewed the workplace the way one might view a hostile, closed, people group living in the 10/40 window. We have thousands of missionaries showing up to our churches on Sundays, and yet we have not given them the proper equipping they need to make disciples in the day-to-day grind.

There are at least two major reasons why:

1. Our church institutional metrics for successful disciple-making are mostly about what happens in the Church Gathered and not where Christians live, work, and play in the Church Scattered.

2. Our church leaders are not any more equipped to train Christians to merge work and faith than the average member is trained to prepare and preach a sermon.

There are plenty of gifted people to fill the training gap if everyone involved is willing to admit that help is desperately needed. The primary purpose of this book is to create a framework that will strategically begin to help all of us work together to equip Christians in discerning God's will and living out their calling. When we believe biblically that our work is part of our worship and that the workplace is the most bountiful mission field in the world, everything changes. When we have this perspective change, the Church Gathered becomes a commissioning for our lives rather than a payoff or an opportunity to check a box.

The Church Scattered movement and ministry model fully integrates faith into every aspect of personal responsibility. In his book, *The Next Christians*, Gabe Lyons puts it this way: "They [Christians] have latched onto one concept and applied it to every area of their lives. Their faith activity isn't restricted to 'religious' activities but carries over into every day of the week and each aspect of their careers, relationships, and social lives."[2]

Lyons goes on to say, "The Christian's faith is quickly losing traction in Western culture, not only as a result of unchristian behavior, as significant as that is, but because we haven't recognized our new reality and adapted."[3]

To help show cultural disruption through time, I've included a list of major cultural shifts in just the last forty years:

CNN launches: 1980
Apple releases Macintosh: 1984
Launch of Internet: 1991
Founding of Amazon: 1994
9/11 Attacks: 2001
Launch of Facebook: 2004
Google goes public: 2004
YouTube makes the world smaller: 2005
First iPhone: 2007
Netflix launches video streaming: 2007
Airbnb disrupts travel industry: 2008
Great Recession: 2008
Uber disrupts travel industry: 2009

We have thousands of missionaries showing up to our churches on Sundays, and yet we have not given them the proper equipping they need to make disciples in the day-to-day grind.

The primary purpose of this book is to create a framework that will strategically begin to help all of us work together to equip Christians in discerning God's will and living out their calling.

First African American president: 2009
#BlackLivesMatter: 2013
Same-sex marriage legalized: 2015
Orlando shooting: 2016
Donald Trump elected president: 2016
#MeToo movement: 2017[4]

When I was in high school, one of the biggest concerns was getting caught smoking in the bathroom. Today, one of the biggest worries is getting shot walking to class.

POSTMODERN

According to Wikipedia, "common targets of postmodernism and critical theory include universalist notions of objective reality, morality, truth, human nature, reason, language, and social progress."

The reality of this for Christianity and the church cannot be overstated. The strategies and methods we have used in North America for decades are no longer going to be effective.

Theologian Stanley Grenz described postmodernism as "a questioning, and even rejection, of the Enlightenment project and the foundational assumptions upon which it was built, namely, that knowledge is certain, objective, and inherently good. Consequently, it marks the end of a single worldview."[5]

This means that even during the instability of the 60s, the cultural context was still committed to a Judeo-Christian worldview. Most people believed there was an absolute truth and moral code that was created by God.

According to Dan Kimball in his excellent book *The Emerging Church*, "Pure modernism held to a single, universal worldview and moral standard, a belief that all knowledge is good and certain, truth is absolute, individualism is valued, and thinking, learning, and beliefs should be determined systematically and logically."[6]

Another critical truth, which is often misunderstood today, is that though the culture is not our enemy, it ultimately is not our friend either.

I grew up in the modern era, which prioritized logic and reason. This, when taken to extremism, leads to humanism and the belief system that supports evolution. After all, if man made God, then we would have to have a systematic structure of truth that could support that conclusion. The postmodern thinkers of our day do not believe there is a single system of truth. Therefore, no truth can be absolute, and collective reasoning is far better than individualistic morality.

According to Barna, whose mission is to help spiritual influencers understand the times and know what to do, "We believe that understanding the reality of this post-truth society and knowing how to wisely respond is more urgent than ever for Christian leaders, parents, and teachers—not just for ourselves but also as we raise up the next generation of Jesus followers."[7]

The somewhat comforting news is that the culture wars we are fighting today have always been parts of the context that Christians must live in. Every generation must continue to navigate and find innovative ways to express eternal truths. Here are a few reminders from the past and predictions about the future:

Just before one of the most divine disruptions in human history—the flood:

> The Lord saw that the wickedness of man was
> great in the earth, and that every intention of the
> thoughts of his heart was only evil continually. And the
> Lord regretted that he had made man on the earth,
> and it grieved him to his heart. (Genesis 6:5-6)

Another one of the many times when the people of God were rejecting his leadership over their lives:

> In those days there was no king in Israel. Everyone did what
> was right in his own eyes. (Judges 21:25)

Finally, clear insight as to where we are headed, if we are not already there:

> But understand this, that in the last days there will come times
> of difficulty. For people will be lovers of self, lovers of money,
> proud, arrogant, abusive, disobedient to their parents, ungrateful,
> unholy, heartless, unappeasable, slanderous, without self-control,
> brutal, not loving good, treacherous, reckless, swollen with conceit,
> lovers of pleasure rather than lovers of God, having the
> appearance of godliness, but denying its power.
> Avoid such people. (2 Timothy 3:1-5)

We need to be careful not to try to play God by determining that it's time to rain down eternal judgment on the people we don't agree with, and therefore have no compassion for. A good reminder:

> The Lord is not slow to fulfill his promise as some count slowness,
> but is patient toward you, not wishing that any should perish,
> but that all should reach repentance. (2 Peter 3:9)

We have been called to be agents for redemption and restoration regardless of how dark the days may become. Because Jesus has commanded us to love our enemies and share with them the good news of the gospel, culture wars should stop, and instead, redemption battles should be fought.

Christians who are fully devoted followers of Christ will seek to use every platform in their lives for building relationships that will lead people toward Christ.

Lyons writes, "I see evidence that the Holy Spirit is working in a new way. He's moving through people where they work and through one-on-one relationships to accomplish great things. They are demonstrating God's love to those around them, not just with words, but in deed."[8]

I absolutely believe the Bible is the inspired Word of God and the guaranteed place to go for all the truth we need about life.

All Scripture is breathed out by God and profitable for teaching,
for reproof, for correction, and for training in righteousness,
that the man of God may be complete, equipped for every good work.
(2 Timothy 3:16-17)

Also, never forget the ministry of the Holy Spirit, who takes the Bible and effectively communicates all the truths we need to be fully devoted followers of Christ and servant leaders of others. When we are not submitted to the Holy Spirit, our Bible knowledge is mere academic babble that distracts from the obedience of the truth we know about the redemption and restoration mandates for every Christian.

A valuable lesson from the great theologian Mark Twain states, "It ain't those parts of the Bible that I can't understand that bother me, it is the parts that I do understand."[9]

The tragic but true contextual reality is that the majority of these three generations believe that the Bible is simply one of many religious books rather than the infallible Word of God; therefore, as a missional strategy, we must understand that relational trust will move generations closer to Christ than propositional truth. Oh no, am I advocating a social gospel here? Absolutely not.

For I am not ashamed of the gospel, for it is the power of God
for salvation to everyone who believes, to the Jew first
and also to the Greek. (Romans 1:16)

With that said, Keller's point must be taken seriously: "We have been allowing culture to disciple our youth for decades; the only difference is that culture isn't on our side anymore. We are the minority."[10]

POST-CHRISTIAN

The most damaging result of the postmodern era is the rejection of absolute truth, especially as it relates to morality and faith. If a person believes and accepts other religious writings as equally authoritative, then they are only one small step from the conclusion of Universalism, which means all paths to God are equal. It is one thing to need to know how to discuss the Bible's trustworthiness, but it is something else entirely when the sufficiency and necessity of Christ's work on the cross is in doubt. This, unfortunately, is the message of cultural evangelist Madonna, who said, "I go to synagogue, I study Hinduism … all paths lead to God."[11]

Let us jump into the deep water of post-Christian culture by reading what Barna has to say: "It may come as no surprise that the influence of Christianity in the United States is waning. Rates of church attendance, religious affiliation, belief in God, prayer and Bible-reading have all been dropping for decades. By consequence, the role of religion in public life has been slowly diminishing, and the church no longer functions with the cultural authority it held in times past. These are unique days for the church in America as it learns what it means to flourish in a new 'Post-Christian' era." [12]

I began to notice these alarming trends in the 1980s when college students who had prioritized church their entire lives stopped attending after graduation. And what's more alarming is that they did not come back to the church once they were married and had started a family.

The cultural disruption exploded in the 1990s, and there was a marked decline in preschool and children's ministry because the next generation of millennials were not attending. We were at the tipping point of moving from a postmodern to post-Christian culture in America.

Barna's research is illuminating. Post-Christian individuals must meet nine or more of the following criteria:

Do not believe in God
Identify as atheist or agnostic
Disagree that faith is important in their lives
Have not prayed to God in the last week
Disagree that the Bible is accurate
Have not donated money to a church in the last year
Have not attended a Christian church in the last six months
Agree that Jesus committed sins
Do not feel personal responsibility to share their faith
Have not read a Bible in the last week
Have not attended a religious small group within the last week
Rank low on Bible engagement scale
Are not born again[13]

"We have been allowing culture to disciple our youth for decades; the only difference is that culture isn't on our side anymore. We are the minority."
- Timothy Keller

If all of this makes you more angry than sad, then you just don't get it. Apart from the grace of God in our own lives as Christians, we would believe and do everything on this list. Why is it that we have more compassion for orphans in Africa than teenagers who live in our cities?

Keller continues with this alarming truth: "Twenty years ago, culture labeled the church as irrelevant. But now culture labels the church as hostile."[14] This means that if you are a part of the younger generation and are considering living for Christ, the majority of your peers and adults will show hostility toward you as well.

During the battle for the Bible in the last century, it was necessary to shift the priority to the truths contained in the Scriptures. If we lost that battle, then we would have also lost the war for redemption and restoration based on God's Word; however, as a result of strongly positioning to the truths of Scripture, we forgot about the messages of God's grace and mercy. We became known in the culture for the things we advocated against rather than the people we were advocating for.

Often in biblical history, people were critical of Jesus for being a friend to sinners and spending too much time with them. Although we are spread thousands of years apart from the time Jesus walked this earth, 21st century Christianity still demands that we learn how to be in the world every day without becoming a part of it.

Sadly, and even unintentionally, leaders of the Church Gathered have, in some situations, created a "holy huddle" dynamic that encourages isolation from lost souls in the culture instead of engagement with them.

In *The Next Christians*, Lyons writes this about the "culture warriors" and their circle-the-wagons approach: "They shout their views at the world and huddle safely with each other—far away from a world they believe is literally going to hell."[15]

This in no way diminishes our responsibility to grow and mature in our faith by pursuing holiness and godliness in everything we do. Being involved in the Church Gathered offers worship and biblical community that are absolutely critical to spiritual growth. On the other hand, if we refuse to be the salt and light that is needed in the Church Scattered, then how can the lost believe in him of whom they have not heard?

Plan "A" for making disciples should be equipping Christians to live out the gospel in the power of the Holy Spirit every day, everywhere, and with everyone.

Along with many other reasons, this fortress mentality is why millennials are rejecting the church. In his book *UnChristian*, David Kinnaman reports, "Our research shows that many of those outside Christianity, especially younger adults, have little trust in the Christian faith, and esteem for the lifestyle of Christ followers is quickly fading among outsiders. They admit their emotional and intellectual barriers go up when they are around Christians, and they reject Jesus because they feel rejected by Christians."[16]

Contextualization demands that we fully understand what the people we are trying to reach believe and why they believe it. It does not demand that we agree with them.

This requires an important leadership life skill if we are going to be effective with helping anyone—our spouse, child, parent, co-worker, or friend. We must be willing to listen with intentions of truly understanding the other person and not listening simply to respond. It is not worth winning the argument based on the facts yet losing the person because we stepped on their heart. For me, this requires compassion for the other person so I can clearly communicate truth with an appropriate measure of grace.

Rachel Held Evans published an important article on CNN called "Why Millennials Are Leaving The Church." She wrote: "What millennials really want from the church is not a change in style but a change in substance. We want an end to the culture wars. We want to be known for what we stand for, not what we are against. We want churches that emphasize an allegiance to the kingdom of God over an allegiance to a single political party or a single nation. We want our LGBT friends to feel truly welcome in our faith communities. We want to be challenged to live lives of holiness, not only when it comes to sex, but also when it comes to living simply, caring for the poor and oppressed, pursing reconciliation, engaging in creation care and becoming peacemakers."[17]

Although I don't agree with everything Evans believes, I find some of her insights applicable. What I am hearing more than anything is that we must seek the right balance of grace and truth for every person and situation.

This is a critical point at the very foundation of the Church Scattered movement. We are not saying that some things are wrong while others are right. I wish it were that easy. What we are saying is that we must shift our priorities in several core areas if we are going to be effective in reaching three entire generations. Preaching and teaching are crucial, but if we don't equip people to learn how to study the Bible for themselves, this battle will be lost.

Dear reader, as you find time to think and pray about the negative and harmful things happening in our culture today, remember this: the darker it gets, the brighter the light will shine.

Jesus reminds us to move beyond the walls of our buildings and into our mission fields in Matthew 5:13-15:

What we are saying is that we must shift our priorities in several core areas if we are going to be effective in reaching three entire generations. Preaching and teaching are crucial, but if we don't equip people to learn how to study the Bible for themselves, this battle will be lost.

You are the salt of the earth, but if salt has lost its taste, how shall its saltiness be restored? It is no longer good for anything except to be thrown out and trampled under people's feet. You are the light of the world. A city set on a hill cannot be hidden. Nor do people light a lamp and put it under a basket, but on a stand, and it gives light to all in the house.

POST-EVANGELISM

This section may prove to be one of the most controversial in the entire book. It is in response to the data about the realities of living in a postmodern and post-Christian American culture and the global disruption that is changing daily.

When we consider the biblical priority of reaching lost people, we are drawn to this classic text:

But you will receive power when the Holy Spirit has come upon you, and you will be my witnesses in Jerusalem and in all Judea and Samaria, and to the end of the earth. (Acts 1:8)

I have heard hundreds of sermons on this passage and, without getting into the meaning of the first century context, let me share the consensus application method. The church, and we as Christians, need to start by reaching people in our Jerusalem. In essence, this means starting with the people who live closest to us and assimilating them into our churches.

The next step of the missions strategy, as it was explained, was to then move outward to the people in Judea, which represents those who live in our cities, but, for example, may live in urban or metropolitan areas.

The third step would be to move from local missions into national missions by developing strategies for the people of Samaria.

Finally, we move into the remotest parts of the earth. This is the realm of international missions, where Christians move to a foreign country with the sole intention of discipling locals. This is where the serious work of cross-cultural missions is done and requires seasoned missions leaders.

When the massive disruption started in the 1980s and people stopped coming to church, I began to pray in earnest seeking to find out why. God led me to Fuller Seminary and The School of World Missions and Church Growth. After seminary, I concluded that the previous model for missions, which I had heard and been taught for years, was no longer a valid way to view the world. This is what I mean by the concept of post-evangelism.

For one simple fact alone, the raging disruptive globalization meant the world was coming together like never before. People from all over the world were moving to America and the movement toward English being spoken globally was dramatic. That, combined with the power of technology, was changing how international missionaries were working globally. For example, The Jesus Film project had total viewings of 5 billion and had been translated over 700 times by the year 2002.

Two other important trends emerged that impacted the Church Scattered and Christianity for the 21st century. First, there was a shift in priority for missionaries leading in foreign countries. Rather than continuing on in these lead missionary roles, they began to equip national leaders to take their place instead.

This may have always been the intent. The ability to calibrate and increase cultural relevance was significantly improved when I noticed that the missionaries were now in the background instead of the pulpits. This transition of major dependency upon the seasoned missions leaders to training the average believers in other countries is the transformation we must see in American churches.

The second trend with similar effectiveness started around the same time in the 1980s. It was called the volunteer missions movement, and the strategy was to get as many church members as possible to attend international missions trips. At first, I thought the primary motive for mission agencies was to give Christians in America a great international experience by seeing God at work in the world. Then, that newfound passion would be shared with the local church upon return. There was hope that this increased awareness would boost financial giving toward missions with an end result of more missionaries being sent out.

Beyond any doubt, the overwhelming majority of Christians are radically changed forever when given the opportunity to do any missions work in which they are able to be the hands and feet of Jesus. For years, I have advocated for all young believers, seminary students, and adults to serve in the city one Sunday per month instead of sitting in a Sunday school classroom.

I experienced this blessing firsthand by going on several mission trips nationally and overseas. The scope of the laity work started in support roles but quickly began to move into direct ministry. Admittedly, this was not as simple as going downtown to volunteer at a rescue mission. There were some real dangers and without proper training, more harm than good could be done to all involved. The value and role of godly missionaries cannot be overstated.

I was on staff with a very large church and to mitigate this risk, it became necessary for a trained professional staff person to lead every international trip to make sure everything went as planned. This again became a constraint, just like the missionary constraint was in the international field.

After much heavy lifting, the day finally came when trained lay leaders were properly prepared for these international trips without a staff member even going. I will never forget the supernatural dynamic of lay leaders working directly with national leaders to plan strategic work within their country

I long for the day when the same dynamic happens in the modern church of America. I see great men and women who are corporate leaders handing out bulletins and making coffee. I understand that from a servant-spirit standpoint, those things are good; however, we have hundreds of people in most of our churches who could help develop a comprehensive strategy for building missional networks and reaching our cities. Honestly, many times the pastors and staff of most churches are simply not equipped to lead them or are too insecure to empower them.

While I was deep into my work at Fuller trying to learn everything I could about missiology, the Church Growth movement was in full swing, and I had the privilege of having Dr. Peter Wagner as my mentor.

When I started my studies at Fuller, the movement was already getting blamed for everything that was wrong with the church. The main target was an inappropriate association with the social gospel, which substituted meeting physical needs for eternal ones. This social justice tension is more of an issue today than ever, and we will deal with it later in the book.

This official statement by The School of World Missions should have put the social gospel issue to rest: "By contrast, I will frequently call attention to classical-biblical mission, by which I mean that a complex of activities whose chief purpose is to make Jesus Christ known as Lord and Savior and to persuade men to become His disciples and responsible members of His church."[18]

The reality was that those leaders framing church growth were far more concerned with the dependency of large urban churches on transfer growth (Christians moving from one church to another) than conversion growth. They actually created a framework for evangelism that would have embarrassed anyone who embraced an attractional-only model for disciple-making.

Their first category of pre-evangelism was Presence. This was social gospel ministry that meant trying to meet both the immediate and biblical needs of caring for the poor.

The second category was Proclamation. The end goal was for people to hear and understand the gospel. To be clear, the preaching of the Word is critical and as written in Isaiah 55, God has promised his Word will not return void.

However, most megachurches put all their eggs in this basket and simply assumed that the Church Growth movement was soft on evangelism. The role of the laity was to invest and invite so the "professionals" could draw the net. The idea of Christians drawing the net where they live, work, and play was preached but never prioritized.

The final category was Persuasion. This topic would shock most professional staff today, and to some degree, be extremely challenging. The Church Growth leaders I worked with believed therefore, knowing the terror of the Lord, we persuade men to repent and be converted, and the only metric for success here was the number of disciples being made.

David Platt sees this same priority for institutional success for too many churches today as bigger crowds, bigger budgets, and bigger buildings. His words are powerful and convicting: "But what is strangely lacking in the picture of performances, personalities, programs, and professionals is desperation for the power of God." [19]

We need to go one step deeper in order to make the major contextual point of this chapter, and quite possibly for the entire book. In Church Growth methodology, scales were developed to distinctly expose the cultural barriers that were in place before unbelievers could be reached.

Here is a form of the modified Engle scale to help with this point of application and is in the context of serving in Memphis in the 1990s at Bellevue Baptist Church. During this time, this congregation was averaging over 5,000 per Sunday.

The scale is comprised of the following and each number represents some type of cultural barrier that must be overcome. The closer the people in the church are culturally to the people in their community, the more effective they will be.

> E-0: No barriers, which translated to white-collar people reaching white-collar people.

> E-1: Megachurches are large enough for white-collar people to reach blue-collar people.

> E-2: They are also large enough to cross racial barriers where members of various ethnicities can minister and fellowship together effectively.

This is ministry representing Jerusalem, Judea, and Samaria for that size church at that time and in that city. Most small churches in Memphis at that time could not be effective in moving beyond E-0 and needed to reach people just like themselves.

I recognize there are many other contextual factors involved here, not the least of which is what the megachurch is able to provide in programming and special events. In 1990, if you had twenty ball fields and excellent children and student programming, you had a clear advantage.

"But what is strangely lacking in the picture of performances, personalities, programs, and professionals is desperation for the power of God."
- David Platt

E-3: This refers to crossing another major barrier such as language or culture. This puts this category and the next one into the "ends of the earth" group. In 1990, this was international missions, and the contexts differed as widely as the massive number of diverse people groups.

Another term that began to be used was cross-cultural missions. If one was trying to reach lost people in Malawi, then all these factors would come into play.

A large amount of missionary training is necessary for any chance of being effective. Can you imagine learning another language and all that is involved in living and working in a third-world culture?

E-4: This is crossing every barrier that is already in place but adding religion to the top of the list. This is working in the 10/40 window where one is trying to reach people who have all of the other barriers, but they are also devout Hindus or Muslims. Everything about their worldview, language, culture, and their beliefs concerning the role of faith in their life must be understood. This group of people is both far from God and far from discipleship opportunities in America as well.

In the 1990s there were two terms that helped define the "reaching" part of the Great Commission. Evangelism, in essence, was reaching people in the E-0, E-1, and E-2 categories and trying to assimilate them into the church. Missions, on the other hand, was the E-3 and E-4 cross-cultural ministry that tried to reach people with the gospel and assimilate them into local churches in their specific areas. All of this was a good strategy for the time, but it does not translate well in modern-day North America.

My conviction is that our present context in America needs to move us from what we would think of as "evangelism" to what we used to think of as "missions." Certainly, I am not advocating the death of evangelism as a personal responsibility of every Christian, but I am saying that Christians who do the work of evangelists need to become missionaries.

Additionally, I believe we have three entire generations of people in America in 2020 that must be reached with an E-3 and E-4 cross-cultural methodology. We left E-0 and E-1 back in Berea, but our evangelical leaders do not own this reality to the degree that they are demanding radical transformation. One of the reasons why is that this would require massive alteration to every institution involved in carrying out the Great Commission. The role of seminaries, denominations, mission agencies, local churches, and, most importantly, individual Christians, must all realign with this new strategy.

We must accept that the people who used to be seen as living in the ends of the earth are now our neighbors and co-workers. It is just as challenging for me to reach my postmodern and post-Christian thirty-year-old neighbor as it would be for me to go to India or Iran and try to reach unbelievers there.

This book cannot resolve all of the implications of these essential changes. I am also fully aware that many people who are smarter and more spiritually mature than I am will disagree with my conclusions, much less my recommendations.

For example, when I work with companies that are being disrupted and their viability is being threatened, they get serious. They must make sure they have the right leaders who have the training necessary to solve the problem. They use these leaders to evaluate their market and then dramatically align their new strategy to meet the present reality.

In our context as evangelical Christians, the leadership development at all levels does not align with the challenges of the present reality. This critical failure can be seen most dramatically when we observe the local church. The pastors and staff are not properly equipped as leaders in order to empower members for ministry in the Church Scattered, and certainly not in a cross-cultural context. The majority of members are biblically illiterate and have absolutely no concept of a calling to be on the front lines of representing God to the world.

To make my point for now, let me share my thoughts on this leadership development crisis. This is an area where I am a practitioner as a Christian, minister, and corporate leader. All that means is that I at least have an informed opinion.

Our seminaries need to dramatically shift their models away from the past. My seminary training was almost exclusively theology-driven with an emphasis on the biblical languages. There was only one required class on missions, and the pastoral leadership was minimal at best. This could have drastically changed by now, but I do not see the results of change in my working with pastors and churches. We need to continue to lay a firm theological foundation, but with an emphasis on ongoing learning and leveraging technology. One phone app today contains more content than my pastoral library in 1990, and it's right at our fingertips.

I strongly advocate that an equal amount of time be given to leadership practices that will equip these key people to be able to deal with everything from leading change to terminating a staff member. We all know from experience that most pastoral failures have more to do with poor leadership than theological disagreements.

The final part of their training should be spent on all of the relevant contextual aspects of missiology. It would be incredibly beneficial to use some of the best practical lessons from all mission agencies and equip these leaders for ministry in modern-day Athens.

It is just as challenging for me to reach my postmodern and post-Christian thirty-year-old neighbor as it would be for me to go to India or Iran and try to reach unbelievers there.

There is one more major application of the post-evangelism era before moving on to the next chapter. This one comes with a personal story that forever changed my approach to reaching lost souls.

I have worked with many evangelists over the years. They have a passion for the lost being saved and are a gift to the church. If they are great at their work, they will never miss an opportunity to share the gospel with someone. I have also been blessed to know several missionaries as well. They also have a passion for lost people coming to Christ. If they are great at their work, they are willing to invest in years of opportunities to see someone come to acknowledge their new identity of "forgiven."

Evangelists are directive when appropriate and are most effective in an E-0 and E-1 context. Missionaries by gifting are more relational and, over the course of years of building trust, are able to reach people who are far from God in an E-3 and E-4 context.

If I am correct that reaching souls in America today is all about cross-cultural missions methodology, then just how dramatically must that revolutionize both our methods and expectations about how we reach unbelievers?

Are pastors willing to have a lost family under their ministry care for years before said family professes Christ as Savior? What about the neighbor or co-worker that may take five years before becoming receptive to hearing a faith story? Even more personal, what about the teenager who is being drug under by sin-riddled influencers and has no interest in God?

When I was at Fuller, there was quite a bit of training on how to discern where someone was on his or her receptivity axis with regard to having a faith conversation. The goal of that training was to learn how to point people to Christ, no matter where a person rests at the time of contact. If a person is receptive and wants to be saved, then a lack of preparation in sharing the gospel would be sinful. On the other hand, if he or she were not ready, and pushed too hard, then they would likely be driven away.

Oh, how dependent we are upon the leadership of the Holy Spirit in these sacred moments:

> *What then is Apollos? What is Paul? Servants through whom you believed, as the Lord assigned to each. I planted, Apollos watered, but God gave the growth. So neither he who plants nor he who waters is anything, but only God who gives the growth. He who plants and he who waters are one, and each will receive his wages according to his labor. For we are God's fellow workers. You are God's field, God's building. (1 Corinthians 3:5-9)*

Working in a cross-cultural setting in America will require more patience, prayer, fasting, and faith than we have ever needed before. It will also require training, wisdom, and discernment to know exactly how to respond in each and every situation.

While working as an executive coach in a corporate setting, I ask each person to fill out an initial assessment form. One of the thirty-plus questions is, "What role does faith play in your life?" I have never had someone not answer, and I know immediately if they are bitter, or angry, or "all in."

I have developed this question contextually after years of experience asking questions that did not work. For example, I previously tried questions like, "Are you a Christian?" "Where do you go to church?" and "Do you know Jesus Christ?" None of these really told me what I needed to know, and, many times, created painful moments for the person involved.

The scale I use today is very simple but extremely important. I have been praying for some people for over thirty years, and I routinely check in to see where they are on their journey. For some, this may be shocking, but for most missionaries, this timeline comes with the territory. I keep records of conversations and make sure to update receptivity regardless of the direction. I want to make sure I align my words and actions with exactly where they need to be in that moment.

The scale looks like this:

> *Hostile: Harmful experiences in the past and are bitter toward God and the church.*
>
> *Negative: Someone or something has hurt them, and they have not forgotten.*
>
> *Indifferent: No interest at all; their mindset is "I don't want to talk about it."*
>
> *Neutral: No strong feelings or thoughts either way.*
>
> *Open: Usually willing to listen but not commit.*
>
> *Interest: Seeking to process faith and hope it will work for them.*
>
> *Receptive: Grateful that God has sent someone to help them find Christ.*

While on staff at Bellevue, I was responsible for leading the Evangelism Explosion training program. At the time, it was the largest in the country. It was by far the most comprehensive training for Christians on how to share their faith that I had ever seen. Because we were working primarily in an E-0 and E-1 context, we saw people pray to receive Christ every week. In that context, we could plow, sow, water, and reap all within an hour conversation.

Working in a cross-cultural setting in America will require more patience, prayer, fasting, and faith than we have ever needed before. It will also require training, wisdom, and discernment to know exactly how to respond in each and every situation.

An experience that changed my life had occurred many years before in my own neighborhood. At the time, I was an "in the ministry" corporate leader who was learning about my sacred calling.

My life changing experience didn't happen within an hour conversation. It started in my own neighborhood where I began learning once again about my sacred calling. One Tuesday night, I decided to take a more intentionally relational approach by visiting one of my neighbors. When this retired railroad engineer answered the door, it was obvious he had been drinking. He was rough and rude. When I told him that I was his neighbor and wanted to invite him to church, it became apparent he was angry with God, and then with me. Determined to not make this another "one and done" visit, I said that I appreciated his time and would be praying for him and his wife. He was caught totally off guard. I then told him I would be back to check on him later and to please let me know if I could ever help as his neighbor. As I began to walk away, I said, "I will be back to see you at a better time." I had heard enough missionary stories and read many books but having never been explicitly taught how to disciple one-on-one made this a challenging and uncertain venture. I prayed daily and remembered that I knew a Christian man who worked for the same railroad. I called my friend and, as it turns out, he knew my neighbor. We talked railroad culture for half an hour.

One month later, I called my neighbor early in the evening. It took a minute for him to connect the dots, but, before he hung up, I asked him if he knew my friend from the railroad. He was immediately more receptive, and we talked for at least fifteen minutes about his work experience. God can work in anyone's heart, but I sincerely believe this contextual effort to relationally connect with him was the key human factor in moving him toward Christ.

Over the next several months, I would call, and we would talk. Sometimes, I would simply inquire about his family's health and ask if there was anything that I could pray over for them. I could sense that his bitterness had begun to melt away.

About a year after our first meeting, I was ready to go back to his home again. I prayed earnestly for the Holy Spirit to soften his heart so he would be receptive to the gospel. When he opened the door, he started crying and said words that I will never forget: "I did not think you would ever really come back." He invited me in, and we sat down at the kitchen table with his wife. After about twenty minutes, he prayed to receive Christ.

For several weeks, we sat at that same kitchen table and I would help him learn as much as possible about walking with Christ daily. I often cried on my walk home at the faithfulness of our gracious God to seek and save another person's life and to use me in the process.

Sometime later, I moved to another city and after a short time we lost touch. I often wondered how he was doing but was too busy with work to take time to reach out. About two years later, we moved back to my hometown. I was invited to a men's event in a church where I was not a member. After walking around for a few minutes, I heard a familiar voice from behind me. It was my former neighbor. We hugged for a long time through lots of tears. Then he offered such life-giving words: "I will never forget that you never gave up on me." Wow!

He introduced me to his pastor and told him our whole story. When the pastor pulled me aside later, he told me that my friend was likely to be ordained as a deacon in the next few months.

I have a heart for people who are far from God. I was once one of the lost, too. I was bitter and angry with God for my mother's death and my father's abuse. When a person comes as far as I have, solely by the grace of God, they realize that there is no one who is beyond the power of the gospel to be rescued and transformed. For rescue to happen, together with the church, we must be willing to revolutionize ourselves first.

My hope is for our passion for Christ to fuel our compassion for others. We cannot pass on to others anything about the Father that we have not first experienced ourselves. At that point, it's all about sharing how good it is to be home with our Father.

DISRUPTIVE TRUTHS

We are now living in a postmodern and post-Christian America that believes there is no absolute truth and many paths to God.

We have three generations in America who are as culturally distant from God as those in the Middle East.

This contextual reality demands a cross-cultural relational approach to effectively reach people for Christ.

We have a leadership development crisis that must be resolved at every level of Christianity.

We have a massive alignment of resource problems that is supporting a failed strategy for making disciples.

Chapter Three: Church Disruption

Ready for some great news? This is the final chapter on disruption. I dare say it won't be the last time we will talk about it, but we're getting close to wrapping up our primary analysis. Now, I want to begin transitioning from defining the problem to discovering what we can do together to solve it.

Since the previous chapters have documented the magnitude of the global and cultural disruptions that are causing a major predicament within the church, there will not be too much statistical data in this chapter. Based on what you've already read, it's likely clear to you that the church is in trouble. Across the board, among all evangelical expressions of the body of Christ, churches are seeing lower numbers in almost every metric that is used to measure success. Even worse, this downward trend has been going on for decades, and there is no end in sight.

In reality, up to one-third of American churches need hospice care. There has been no growth in thirty plus years, so they simply linger until the remaining senior adults pass away.

As Charles Arn says, "The longer a church exists, the more concerned the leaders and members become with self-service, and the less concerned with the church's original mission and reason for being."[1]

However, we should help churches by prayerfully suggesting that they potentially merge with other churches, give their property to other church plants, or, at a minimum, sell their property and give the money to mission organizations.

Alarmingly, up to another third of all churches, though they do not yet require hospice care, have not grown in years. These churches have plateaued, and if something very radical is not done soon, they will perish as well. These churches are ripe for disruption.

Mark Deymaz lists several characteristics of churches that are ripe for disruption:

>   1.) A disconnect exists between past and present effectiveness.
>
>   2.) A considerable drop in attendance has led to a loss of stability, capacity, and direction in a congregation once known for its size and significance.
>
>   3.) An environment of high control and poor communication has the staff confused and complaining.

4.) A senior pastor is prone to make excuses or to blame others for personal shortcomings or lack of success within the church rather than accept constructive criticism meant to help.

5.) A mindset of scarcity, rather than abundance, governs the thinking of leaders averse to risk and unwilling to fund new initiatives.

6.) A neighborhood has changed, but rather than embrace the possibilities, the church is determined to remain the same in terms of race, class, or culture.

7.) A revolving door exists through which both paid and lay leaders are constantly coming and going.[2]

I applaud all the work that people like Thom Rainer and others are doing to try to revitalize and even replant many of these churches. Rainer says, "Nine out of ten churches in North America are declining, or they are growing slower than the community in which they are located."[3] I pray for their success, but I also realize the challenges they are facing are extremely difficult.

Although one-third of churches are in need of intensive care and another third have plateaued, the promising news is that potentially up to one-third of American churches are also showing signs of health and growth. They are as diverse in methodology as they are in their style of worship music. This diversity is being driven by the necessity of contextualization for effectiveness. In the past, a few megachurches would host conferences and endorse their methodology, and all other churches would attend and assume they should model that methodology. I know these conferences still exist, but there is an irreversible movement in place that communicates that one ministry plan does not fit all today. Smaller churches are finally progressing because this culture appreciates the relational community.

Major denominations are in even worse condition because of the failures of the institutional culture that often values its reputation over the needs of its people. This does not apply to all, but massive leadership change is needed.

The major disruptive truth of this chapter is that Jesus—the founder, owner, and leader of the church—is undoubtedly disrupting it down to the foundation. No new programming emphasis or live streaming technology is going to be adequate this time.

Radical transformation will require repentance and obedience. We have lost our first love and until we restore Christ to his rightful place of preeminence, nothing supernatural will be sustainable. We have moved beyond conviction, testing, and pruning into full blown divine chastisement. We have quoted for years, "Judgment

> **The major disruptive truth of this chapter is that Jesus—the founder, owner, and leader of the church—is undoubtedly disrupting it down to the foundation. No new programming emphasis or live streaming technology is going to be adequate this time.**

must first begin at the house of God," and now we are living it.

Even as I write this, I know I have contributed to the problem as a spiritually imma-ture Christian who cared more about living the American dream than lifting up the kingdom of God. I have been a church leader who joyfully watched the attendance numbers go up, but I knew in my spirit that something was broken.

Too many people have had to pay a painful price while we prioritized the wrong things. On the other hand, I have never been more excited and hopeful than I pres-ently am for the future of the church. When the Church Gathered and the Church Scattered fully embrace the mission of representing God to the world, eternal things will start to happen beyond anything we could ask, hope, or think. The pain of the present will be replaced by our greater hope for the future.

Since I have had to take far too many trips to the Father's proverbial woodshed in my personal Christian life, I will remind all of us of this incredible truth:

> The Spirit himself bears witness with our spirit that we are children of God,
> and if children, then heirs--heirs of God and fellow heirs with Christ,
> provided we suffer with him in order that we may also
> be glorified with him. For I consider that the sufferings of this
> present time are not worth comparing with the glory
> that is to be revealed to us. (Romans 8:16-18)

As we have already mentioned, divine disruption is an ongoing theme in the Bible. From the floods of Noah to the fires of Sodom and Gomorrah, God has dramati-cally brought radical change through his judgment. From the period of the judges and the kings, we see the vicious cycle of God's blessing and extended mercy, only to be met with thanklessness and disobedience. This type of performance-based relationship with God is still alive and thriving in the church of the 21st century.

When the wrath comes, the "repentance" follows, but only temporarily. We love coming together and building towers for our own glory, and God keeps scattering us in hopes we will live for his instead.

These cycles of God's gathered people needing to be scattered again were nothing new to the New Testament period, either. Almost immediately after the crucifixion, resurrection, commissioning, ascension, empowering of the Holy Spirit, and the birth of the early church, divine scattering was needed again:

> And Saul approved of his execution. And there arose on that day
> a great persecution against the church in Jerusalem, and they
> were all scattered throughout the regions of Judea and Samaria,
> except the apostles. Devout men buried Stephen and made

When the Church Gathered and the Church Scattered fully embrace the mission of representing God to the world, eternal things will start to happen beyond anything we could ask, hope, or think.

great lamentation over him. But Saul was ravaging the church,
and entering house after house, he dragged off men and women
and committed them to prison. Now those who were
scattered went about preaching the word.
Philip went down to the city of Samaria and proclaimed
to them the Christ. (Acts 8:1-5)

Please don't miss the connection between persecution, scattering, and preaching, followed by conversions shortly thereafter. This may be the exact same strategy that God has been using all over the world for centuries. Now, it is our turn in America.

Both the gathering and scattering of the church are good things, unless we prioritize one and minimize the other. If that happens, then we fail to accomplish the mission of making disciples.

"Holy huddles" and virtual churches are not part of the strategy of God for his church to represent him to the world. However, true biblical community is sacred space and there should never be guilt over watching another teacher on "Right Now Media."

CHURCH CONTEXTUALIZATION 2020

As I mentioned earlier, the culture is not our enemy, nor is it our friend. The modern worldview of the 19th and 20th centuries interpreted the Scriptures through the lenses of science, logic, and reason. They rejected an authoritative view of the Bible, and most of that period for the church was spent rejecting this false teaching. We are still facing some of these same issues today, but we are doing so through the lens of a 21st century culture that has even more problems with absolute truth.

Before we analyze the present any further, let's be faithful to remember what God has already done by taking a look at how God has been reforming his church for the last fifty years. I think pastors and church staff will find this chapter especially valuable, but it is also for Christians who are struggling to figure out why the Church Gathered is no longer working for them anymore.

For the most part, back in the 1990s, there was one basic type of evangelical church. There were plenty of liberal expressions, but most Christians could see those differences and make the best decision for their family. The primary distinctions during that time were not radically different approaches about preaching style, music genre, small groups, or missions; however, presently the contextual factor for Christians means there are twenty different expressions of the body of Christ to choose from—not just one based on size.

The disruptive factor in the 80s and 90s was the rise of the megachurch and its impact on other churches and Christians. A spiritual version of Wal-Mart had just moved into town, and this was bad news for all the smaller versions still trying to compete for the same people.

When competing with Starbucks-style coffee shops, state-of-the-art fitness facilities, Disney-like children's programming, and a worship experience that rivals a Coldplay concert, the attractional advantage is overwhelming. Sadly, many of these dying churches in large urban cities could not recover.

Hear me clearly: I have spent thirty years helping to lead and leverage megachurches, and I am not ready to shut them down or declare they are harmful to the kingdom of God. Certainly, they have their own set of competitive issues concerning these three generations, and, now, they, like all the brick and mortar malls, are in desperate need of a new strategy.

One of the biggest regrets I have is that we as leaders of these megachurches did not do more to help the smaller gatherings of the body of Christ be successful. I have good news for everyone: smaller is no longer at an extreme disadvantage when the incredible power of the Church Scattered is harnessed.

Another regret is that because we were so blinded by the numerical growth, we wrongly assumed that by offering the best class programming, disciples were being made and the Great Commission fulfilled. These missteps led to the development of a powerful, co-dependent culture that met the misguided expectations of church leaders and committed Christians. The megachurch was successful because there was numerical growth, and members loved outsourcing parenting and Bible study to others.

Christians today must understand why God is disrupting his church. We must ask ourselves hard questions like, "Why are we members of this church?" and "Why do we struggle every week to even want to go?" As we wrestle with the answers, we must remember that dynamic is on us and not the church leaders. If our answers indicate consumer-driven Christianity, we first need to dramatically change our spiritual priorities, and then we will be able to see clearly if we should stay or go. As I mentioned earlier, unless we are getting more out of the Word on our own than through others, we will not grow spiritually.

One dramatic shift most churches are adopting relates to children's ministry. Back in the 90s, the culture supported most Christians going to the Church Gathered for six to ten hours per week. It was easy to understand why most Christian parents thought that was enough. However, when all the postmodern cultural changes kicked in, church leaders finally realized that if parents of these new generations hand over their children twice a month for two hours max, the church could no longer be expected to have the primary responsibility for their spiritual character formation because time simply wasn't on their side.

Initially, these changes were based more on pragmatism than theology. Then God, because of this divine disruption, raised up leaders like Reggie Joiner, who founded Orange, a ministry designed to commission parents to reclaim the primary role of discipleship and to equip churches to come alongside them.

Now, to be effective, a church's role on Sundays is to help set up parents for success in the Church Scattered world of kitchen tables and carpool. They should develop the resources and push these resources to parents in an accessible way, and then parents must invest the time to leverage every interaction.

To be blunt, I would never join a church that tried to shift that responsibility back to the church and away from the parents. These churches are trying to create dependency instead of empowerment.

But, when the responsibility shifts from the church to the individuals, what does that mean for preaching and teaching in the Church Gathered? Is it still valuable? Absolutely. However, we must begin to view this equipping as a "setup" for the work before us and not the "payoff" for the week behind us.

When we view Sunday's sermon as a payoff served up by an incredibly gifted communicator, when it's over, we will feel as if we just devoured a five-course meal—full and satisfied. However, by Sunday night, we begin to feel hungry again. If all we have to sustain us is devotional "snacks" every morning, we will run out of spiritual margin by noon on Monday.

If, on the other hand, Sunday's sermon is the setup for the week ahead, then we leave our Sunday experience equipped, inspired, convicted, and challenged to live our week on mission for Christ. We consider it our responsibility to own our spiritual maturity and that of our family.

When leaders cast this kind of vision for both the Church Gathered and Church Scattered, members now have a calling and not just a career. The dependency that is created is on the daily power of the Holy Spirit and not the weekly programming of the church. For this reason, I would not join a church where there was more emphasis on celebrity leaders building a following than there was on scattering missionaries. When you hear leaders endorse the church establishment more than they endorse Christ, that may be a sign that they just don't get it.

Before we look at all the positive reformations God is creating in his church, let me address one more thing. Just a warning—this one hurts more than the other two.

Active church attendance and serving every week can be an extremely dangerous thing for your spiritual health and even your marriage. Church staffs can become obsessed with making sure they have enough workers in every area each week.

On the surface, this is a biblically sound priority because we have all been given spiritual gifts to serve and benefit the body. Also, serving is a critical piece of the spiritual formation process. However, the question that every church leader should be asking is, "What is best for each volunteer or family?" and not "How can volunteers help us get the work done?" The reality is that many couples will serve every week to avoid intimacy and accountability in group life.

For example, Christians enduring the pain of a failing marriage may find a safe hiding space in the church and in their children. They may become blinded to the truth that the healing of their marriage is always what's best for their church and their children. These couples don't need service opportunities and shiny kids' ministry activities as much as they need the deep, personal ministry they might receive from a small group.

Additionally, growing Christians may need to be in a class learning how to study their Bibles instead of running the lights for the service. We have to find ways to assess where people are spiritually and discern what they need the most. I missed that responsibility and deeply regret it.

Unfortunately, church can be the perfect place to balance out this guilt and mask personal pain. We must stop looking primarily at activity to indicate spiritual health, and, instead, we must start providing safe places for hurting people.

Marriage is exhibit A for the gospel and it is almost entirely lived out in the Church Scattered. We cannot be more concerned with getting VBS workers than creating relationships in which love and respect are given and received.

I would not join a church that places more emphasis on getting people plugged in to service than they do on building healthy families. I long for the day when church leaders assume the responsibility of being the "setup" for this priority instead of hiring more counselors.

CHURCH GROWTH MOVEMENT 1970

The year 1970 shows that the church and Christians have been struggling for a long time in their mission to represent God to the world. This movement should have been a disruption instead of a mere realignment.

In Donald McGavran's foundational book *Understanding Church Growth*, he writes the following: "Faithful obedience to Jesus Christ as Lord implies bending all efforts, energies, and resources above all in bringing men and women to follow Christ in true discipleship, and to join themselves together in the fellowship of local churches. If tens are being won where thousands could and should be won, that particular strategy fails the test."[4]

Marriage is exhibit A for the gospel and it is almost entirely lived out in the Church Scattered. We cannot be more concerned with getting VBS workers than creating relationships in which love and respect are given and received.

It is critical to understand that this movement was started and sustained for many years by missionaries. They were absolutely trying to apply the methods used in their cross-cultural E-3 and E-4 ministry in a North American context.

It was assumed by most evangelical leaders at this time that the battle for the Bible was more important than making major changes to church methodology. They were probably right about that.

There was also the rise of the religious right and the hope that our prevailing Judeo-Christian worldview would prevail over the onslaught of liberalism. There was a strong emphasis put on the idea that political and governmental reforms would lead to moral change. Remember that the emergence of megachurches gave the illusion that many disciples were being made. So, at the time, the disruptive words of the missionaries were dismissed as purely academic.

The lesson for every Christian is that God is always trying to use his Word and other people to express his truth to us. He is never silent, but we have to reduce all other noise to be able to hear him.

PURPOSE DRIVEN CHURCH 1995

Rick Warren's book was so revolutionary, it had to be disruptive. Here is a taste of the radical things he was saying:

> "The key issue for churches in the 21st century will be church health, not church growth." [5]

> "I believe that you measure the health or strength of a church by its sending capacity rather than its seating capacity."[6]

> "We do not want transfer growth. In membership class we say, 'If you are coming to Saddleback from another church, you need to understand up front that this church was not designed for you. It is geared toward reaching the unchurched who do not attend anywhere.'"

> "If you are transferring from another church you are welcome here only if you are willing to serve and minister. If all you intend to do is attend services, we'd rather save your seat for someone who is an unbeliever."[7]

> "Never confuse methods with the message. The message must never change, but the methods must change with each new generation."[8]

> "I contend that when a church continues to use methods that no longer work, it is being unfaithful to Christ."[9]

Although the majority of pastors and church leaders would agree with most of what he was promoting, they would never take the risk of putting their leadership credibility on the line beyond a sermon or staff conversation.

Warren's intentionality to attend to both the reaching and equipping responsibilities of the church was incredible. He purposely moved unchurched people from the community into the crowd of involvement with members and ministry. He also created a required membership class and a highly developed spiritual growth process that actually measured progress. He said, "If I were to use business terms, I'd say that our church is in the 'disciple-development' business and that our product is changed lives—Christlike people."[10]

To this day, Warren is one of the greatest leaders, pastors, missionaries, evangelists, and Christians I have ever met. If you have not read *Purpose Driven Life*, you have missed one of the greatest personal leadership books ever written.

Why then was Warren's work rejected by so many when it was exactly what we needed to hear and do? For starters, Warren and I attended Fuller at the same time, and that alone could put one in the proverbial doghouse of evangelical leadership.

Consider how different he was from other pastors: he started a church with multiple services, in a school of all places. He dressed down in the pulpit. His communication style was more "teaching" than "preaching." People complained that his sermons were way too much application and not enough exposition.

The irony of this is that if Warren was conducting church this way in South America as a missionary, he would have been honored by any conservative group for his devotion and effectiveness in ministry. (Even though we all know California has its issues, this is still North America.)

Underneath the problems we are facing in 2020, there is a deeper problem that must be addressed: something I call "neocolonialism."

The technical definition of colonialism is a policy by which a nation maintains or extends its control over foreign dependencies. Let's modify that some to fit our context: a policy by which an institution maintains or extends its control over its dependencies. That means that the success of the institution itself is seen as more important than meeting the needs of the people it was intended to serve. To this day, the "American Church" is seen by many as a vital institution that must be protected at all costs.

I recall the shocking image I saw in a picture promoting foreign missions over forty years ago. It was a man in a remote part of Africa standing under a tree, dressed in a suit with a Baptist hymnal in his hand. At that time, we church leaders thought

The institutions that support the "American Church" are powerful forces, and they will resist disruption at all costs. They, like the Apostle Peter, will eat with anyone until it threatens their role within the institution.

the most effective thing to do for reaching these people was to make "American Christians" out of them. The only way to do that was for them to come to Christ the same way we did and then to become just like us.

I know what you're thinking: today, surely all of this type of thinking is dead, and we are open to reaching people who are different from us in a culturally relevant, but biblical way. Well, that depends greatly on context.

For example, today I have seen thousands of Christians go on these same trips to Africa and actually sing, dance, and wave their hands in heartfelt worship with their fellow believers. Then, they come back home only to blow up on the student minister because the music is way too loud and the dress code is severely lacking.

The institutions that support the "American Church" are powerful forces, and they will resist disruption at all costs. They, like the Apostle Peter, will eat with anyone until it threatens their role within the institution.

The application for every Christian is that we must be intentional and proactive to set the personal priorities that God has for our lives. Bottom line: trust the Holy Spirit to lead you more than institutional leaders.

THE EMERGING CHURCH 2003

This book was written within the context of a postmodern and post-Christian culture, which shifts our methodology toward a missional mindset. Dan Kimball knows we are now in full-blown disruption. He writes, "As we serve in a post-Christian mission field, we need to use the same approach we would employ entering a foreign culture. We cannot go on seeing ourselves simply as pastors and teachers; we need to see ourselves as a new kind of missionary (bi-vocational faith and work)."[11]

According to Kimball, the church has clearly become more of a place than a people. Essentially, the programs that people are attending can easily take priority over the mission they should be accomplishing. Notice his sharp contrasts between an inwardly focused church compared to one that is living and working in its mission field every day:

> *Consumer Church*: Church is seen as a dispenser of religious goods and services. People come to church to be fed, to have their needs met through quality programs, and to have the professionals teach their children about God.

> *Missional Church*: Church is seen as a body of people sent on a mission who gather in community for worship, encouragement, and teaching from the Word that supplements what they are feeding themselves throughout the week.[12]

Are you noticing over and over again the absolute necessity of a full integration of faith into every area of your life? The other concept that cannot be missed is that individual Christians living and working in the Church Scattered must take priority over the ministry of the Church Gathered.

I could not agree more with Kimball's insightful request to the Father, "My prayer is that we will have the courage to stay true to the Scriptures while radically rethinking the way we do ministry. May we seize this moment in history and become missionaries again, being sensitive to post-Christian culture, living lives of intense dependence on the Spirit, and rethinking what the church will be for new generations."[13]

SIMPLE CHURCH 2006

One of the lasting negative impacts of the megachurch movement is that too many churches are trying to do too many things. It is still assumed that the more things that are done, the more positive results will follow.

This mistake is made in corporate culture every day. Once-successful organizations that did some things extremely well over-reached into areas where they had no real competency or competitive advantage. In their world, it was always assumed that any additional revenue was a good thing. So, according to their way of thinking, bigger meant better, and it satisfied the stock market by moving the numbers.

However, with all the additional revenue came increased cost. Although the top-line numbers were consistently going up, the bottom-line profit margins were falling. Worse than that, the new undertakings did not align with the quality existing ones, and so they became a mile wide and an inch deep. The final result of this downward spiral is losing the competitive advantage once associated with the original brand.

McDonald's tried to be everything to everyone, and now, though their menus are large, nothing they sell tastes good anymore. General Electric was once one of the most iconic brands in the world, but now they are selling anything they can just to survive.

Strategic leadership training will drive home the point that every great leader must be willing to make tradeoffs. You identify your core priorities and say "no" to everything else.

Simple Church leaders have the courage to say "no" to all of the different priorities constantly flowing up from the members. For them, "focus is the commitment to abandon everything that falls outside of the simple ministry process. Focus most often means saying 'no.' Focus requires saying, 'yes' to the best and 'no' to everything else." [14]

"As we serve in a post-Christian mission field, we need to use the same approach we would employ entering a foreign culture. We cannot go on seeing ourselves simply as pastors and teachers; we need to see ourselves as a new kind of missionary (bi-vocational faith and work)."- Dan Kimbell

> **"**
>
> *The cancerous myth of "bigger is better" has drastically impacted the church in North America. We falsely believed the bigger the buildings, budgets, programming, staff, and attendance, the more successful we must be. Tragically, no one was watching the real impact on the bottom line.*

The cancerous myth of "bigger is better" has drastically impacted the church in North America. We falsely believed the bigger the buildings, budgets, programming, staff, and attendance, the more successful we must be. Tragically, no one was watching the real impact on the bottom line.

This dynamic plays out in our personal and family life more than anywhere else. Because we have not defined the non-negotiable, we are not able to say "no" to the urgent, and we leave the important undone.

I believe our major regrets in life will not come from all of the mistakes we have made, but because of the opportunities we missed. That is why our families live in a constant state of exhaustion, and, as parents, we often feel guilty.

When Thom Rainer and Eric Geiger wrote *Simple Church*, it was disruptive because it challenged the idea that more is better. After much research, they actually reached the opposite conclusion that it may, in reality, be worse. They found that, "the healthiest churches in American tended to have a simple process for making disciples. They had clarity about the process. They moved Christians intentionally through the process. They were focused on the elements of the process. And they aligned their entire congregation to this process."[15]

This clearly documented that an intentional discipleship process is at the heart of solving the crisis of disciple-making. The expression in corporate culture that says, "If you don't measure it then it must not matter" could never be more relevant.

These metrics must include priorities that exist in the Church Scattered. They can include prayer, Bible study, meals together, and intentional conversations with non-believers. With technology tools like Survey Monkey, the customization is perfect for contextualization and you can easily get feedback from members on progress.

Notice the important contrast: "Simple Church leaders are designers. They design opportunities for spiritual growth. Complex Church leaders are programmers. They run ministry programs."[16]

Complex Church leaders are great with what, how, and who on any given ministry, but they have forgotten the most important issue of why. This dynamic also exhausts those on staff and lay leadership teams who are simply trying to keep up.

One of the most powerful words in corporate culture today is "alignment." Leaders must make sure the vision is clear, the people are trained, and the culture is empowering.

These same dynamics are in place with Simple Church culture: "the leadership and the church are clear about the process and are committed to executing it. The process flows logically and is implemented in each area of the church. The church abandons everything that is not in the process."[17]

This process can be seen in the following four major areas:
1. Clarity: Starting with a Ministry Blueprint
2. Movement: Removing Congestion
3. Alignment: Maximizing the Energy of Everyone
4. Focus: Saying No to Almost Everything

The Simple Church model prioritizes leadership development, which must be in place for all of our churches to be successful. When everyone knows why, the bottom line becomes the only metric that matters.

An absolute critical priority is that all of the leaders in the church are walking their talk. If you are talking about the priority of developing personal relationships with lost people yet have no personal stories to share, you have no credibility. When church leaders are not moving in the same direction, eventually everyone will know it. When the stories are coming from both the Church Gathered and the Church Scattered, your city will know it as well.

For Simple Church leaders, "the goal is to partner with God to move people through the stages of spiritual growth. Changed lives are the bottom line, the intended end result. Christ formed in people is the goal."[18]

TRANSFORMATIONAL CHURCH 2010

Please don't miss the divine progression here over the last fifty years. As I said at the beginning of this book, the only solution for disruption is transformation. We have now moved from Church Growth, to Purpose Driven Church, to Emerging Church, to Simple Church, and finally, to Transformational Church.

Transformational Church by Ed Stetzer and Thom Rainer brought me to the place of developing the Church Scattered strategy. I owe so much about what I currently believe to their incredible work. They deal with almost all of my disruptive truths in this book, and they understand we are in a cross-cultural context and nothing short of the integration of the secular and sacred will resolve our disrupted methodology. Until we have the full integration of leadership/life, faith/work, Christianity/calling, and church/mission, we will not have addressed Christianity for the 21st century.

I believe our major regrets in life will not come from all of the mistakes we have made, but because of the opportunities we missed.

I will use more quotes in this section than normal. The first reason is, the original authors can say it better than I can. Secondly, they deserve the credit for challenging us on all of these critical insights.

"Transformational churches make disciples whose lives are being transformed by the gospel, so that the culture around them is ultimately transformed. They practice and make disciples through vibrant leadership, prayerful dependence, and relational intentionality in their context with a missionary mindset."[19]

I submit that this statement could be used in training any missionary who is going to serve anywhere in the world as a formula for success. Hopefully, our evangelical institutions will believe and embrace this truth and radically change their role in the kingdom.

If we study the New Testament, it's clear that key leadership should be placed in the local church and not in any denominational hierarchy. Radically redefining the roles of the clergy and laity is just the beginning, as all of us become Christian missionaries. If the church does not step up and assume its responsibility, then individual Christians must.

One of the most staggering statements in the book reads, "Too often the church has become a symbol of gathering for one another rather than scattering for the sake of others. The church was designed by God to be on the move in the world, not sitting in the corner of the neighborhood waiting for the needs to show up on its doorstep."[20]

It is not possible to read that statement, if you believe it is true, and not reach the conclusion that the number one strategy of God to reach the world is Christians living out their faith every day. We have been conditioned to think that the going in the Great Commission is akin to taking an international mission trip.

We go on these mission trips with extreme intentionality to do everything we can to share the good news of the gospel with everyone we meet. We become a completely different person in that context, and we experience Christ more fully than ever before. However, when we return home, we descend from our mountaintop experience and return to our normal lives of work, marriage, parenting, and church attendance. Please hear me: there should be no return. You are indwelt by the Spirit of God to be empowered to live out the mission of God.

I want to continue the conversation about the role of social justice for Christians and the church in the 21st century. It is both one of our most difficult challenges and greatest opportunities in reaching these three generations in North America. The reason it is a challenge is because we must not stop with ministries of restoration that do not lead to redemption. It will never be enough to simply give someone food and water hoping this act of common grace is sufficient for leading them to salvation.

Consider these two very compelling passages of Scripture:

*Jesus said to them, "I am the bread of life; whoever comes
to me shall not hunger, and whoever believes in me
shall never thirst." (John 6:35)*

*Jesus said to her, "Everyone who drinks of this water
will be thirsty again, but whoever drinks of the water that I
will give him will never be thirsty again. The water that I will give
him will become in him a spring of water welling up
to eternal life." (John 4:13-14)*

I have reached the conviction that social justice without eternal redemption is not really justice at all. On the other hand, I struggle with the other biblical perspective that any eternal redemption that does not lead to social justice is not redemption at all.

When we as Christians become more concerned with politics, legislation, and the restoration of America than we are building the kingdom, we have surrendered our role in God's redemptive plan. While we are called to obey these laws of the land, the gospel is the only power of God that transforms, and we must never confuse the means with the end.

I may have to let the theologians settle this, right after they figure out the sovereignty of God and the responsibility of man conundrum. Whatever the answer, I fully agree with the following that talks about the roles of Christians and the church: "It is about reaching a critical mass of believers who are so empowered by the gospel of Christ that they change everything they touch—family, workplace, schools, business. As this critical mass is achieved, the power of God brings significant changes in the problems that plague our cities today—poverty, crime, addictions, gangs, divorce, violence—and a dramatic increase in things that characterize the kingdom of God—mercy, justice, prosperity for poor and compassion."[21]

This statement reflects not only the challenge but the great opportunity before us: when lost people in this culture experience the reality of Jesus Christ through their interactions with transformed Christians where they live, work, and play, they will be changed.

I absolutely love this quote from Dietrich Bonhoeffer: "Your life as a Christian should make nonbelievers question their disbelief in God."[22] Let's pray as we care for the hurting, sick, widowed, and orphaned that all will see the hands and feet of Jesus and not our own.

One of the critical findings in Stetzer and Rainer's work is the importance of changing the scorecard on how churches measure success. The old scorecard only measured things that primarily happened at the Church Gathered.

You are indwelt by the Spirit of God to be empowered to live out the mission of God.

The old scorecard:

1. ...counts the number of dollars being used and the number of square feet being inhabited for the purpose of the church. Bodies, budgets, and buildings.

2. ...keeps us church-absorbed. As long as we use it, we will continue to be inward-focused, program-driven, and church-based in our thinking and leadership.

3. ...is based on a brick-and-mortar mentality that reinforces the church as a specific time and place occurrence.[23]

It's crucial to see that this way of measuring success not only doesn't work, but it reinforces an unhealthy culture. We must start measuring Church Scattered desired outcomes like personal Bible study, prayer, and intentional conversations with lost people.

In his book *Missional Renaissance*, Reggie McNeal states it this way:

"When the church thinks it's the destination, it also confuses the scorecard. It thinks that if people are hovering around and in the church, the church is winning. The truth is, when that is the case the church is keeping people from where they want to go, from their real destination. The destination is life...Abundant life is lived out with loved ones, friends, and acquaintances in the marketplace, in the home, in the neighborhood, in the world."[24]

So, based on everything shared, should we determine that the Church Gathered is not as important as it used to be? Absolutely not. In fact, it is more important today than ever.

Should we then continue to consider the Church Gathered as the primary way that God wants to help us grow spiritually? Absolutely not. The Church Gathered is the setup for the ministry before us, not the payoff for the week behind us.

As I mentioned in the introduction, the major challenge facing us today is not with the Church Gathered but Christians living out their faith in the Church Scattered. We cannot blame the church establishment for our broken marriages, failing children, and overstressed lives.

This will be a shock for most of us because we still have way too much performance-based theology in our head. We still believe to some degree that if we do good things for God then he in turn will do good things for us. This mentality is born out of spiritual immaturity caused by thinking that listening to the truth is the same as living it. Nothing could be further from the truth.

66

"Your life as a Christian should make nonbelievers question their disbelief in God.
- Dietrich Bonhoeffer

I have done much work creating the new scorecard, and I have leveraged technology to evaluate the spiritual maturity of many active Christians. For example, I will ask people to respond to the following question.

> 1.)How important is reading the Bible to your spiritual growth?
> a. Not at all
> b. Somewhat
> c. Very
> d. Extremely

This represents what they believe based on years of hearing this truth in many different Church Gathered settings. The next question is about the payoff.

> 2.) How often do you read your Bible during the week?
> a. Never
> b. Seldom
> c. Often
> d. Daily

This represents not what they believe, but how they behave. James would call us out by saying "show me your faith by your works."

I have been devastated by the consistent answers that I have received from so many active in the Church Gathered. They, like many church leaders, have incorrectly assumed that years of church attendance has made them disciples.

Over 80 percent will identify with reading the Bible as "very" or "extremely" important to their spiritual growth, but the same group will then admit that they "never" or "seldom" read the Bible during the week.

> But be doers of the word, and not hearers only, deceiving yourselves.
> For if anyone is a hearer of the word and not a doer, he is like a man
> who looks intently at his natural face in a mirror. For he looks at
> himself and goes away and at once forgets what he was like. But the
> one who looks into the perfect law, the law of liberty, and perseveres,
> being no hearer who forgets but a doer who acts, he will be blessed
> in his doing. (James 1:22-25)

This reality absolutely changed my expectations about the role of the church in my life. I used to be so disappointed or even angry when the music, message, or lesson was not what I needed that week. Why was I disappointed and angry? Because I had placed the wonderful Church Gathered ministry not only in the primary priority slot, but in the only slot. When we are dependent upon other people feeding us for a week, and they don't, bad things start to happen.

The Church Gathered is the setup for the ministry before us, not the payoff for the week behind us.

As I began to grow spiritually, another personal reality set in. My emphasis was still on learning truth and not living it. After years of reading through the Bible, I finally realized that something was very wrong. I had heard hundreds of sermons, and even more lessons about the Bible, but I experienced no noticeable change in my marriage, parenting, or work. Then, the Book of Hebrews took me beyond where I had been in James.

> *For though by this time you ought to be teachers, you need someone to teach you again the basic principles of the oracles of God. You need milk, not solid food, for everyone who lives on milk is unskilled in the word of righteousness, since he is a child. But solid food is for the mature, for those who have their powers of discernmentt rained by constant practice to distinguish good from evil. (Hebrews 5:12-14)*

The end goal was clear to me now. Opening the Word of God or listening to it without a full commitment to obey what it says is a dangerous place to be.

DISRUPTIVE TRUTHS

God is intentionally scattering his Church to empower Christians to live out their faith every day.

Churches and denominations are failing at an alarming rate and something transformational must be done.

The primary responsibility for the spiritual formation process does not belong to the church, but to individual Christians.

The traditional scorecard for church success is no longer adequate, and new Church Scattered metrics must be developed.

The church must have a process of disciple-making that is intentional, and it must be willing to say "no" to almost everything else.

Christians must understand that learning the Bible is never a substitute for living it.

Chapter Four: Great Omission

I wish I could write this chapter entirely through my tears to be able to convey how deeply I desire for you to understand just how much Jesus Christ loves you.

Our calling and mission in life is to know Christ and make him known to the world. I can't believe we are given the honor of doing this.

I need to take you back to that meeting in the corporate boardroom and share all that God was doing in my life during that time. The progression of truth about knowing him has been consistent over the years, and I want you to be able to apply my journey into your life.

I never went to church, but always believed in God. I assumed that when I died there would be a final audit of my life. As long as the good outweighed the bad, then I would be going to heaven. This is the dominant view of most major religions in the world today and many members of the next generation.

It was quite a shock to me when I heard that this was not how eternity would play out. Salvation would not be based on all the good I had done for God, but all that Christ had done for me.

> *For by grace you have been saved through faith. And this is not your own doing; it is the gift of God, not a result of works, so that no one may boast. (Ephesians 2:8-9)*

Because I also grew up in a home with no mother, and where my father never once told me he loved me, I was starved for someone who really cared. In the process of coming to Christ, stories like the love of the Father for the prodigal son would bring me to tears. The reality that the Father would offer mercy to me instead of the justice I deserved, broke my heart. With extreme gratitude, I trusted in Christ's death on the cross as the full and final payment for all of my sin. Because he went "all in" for me, I would gladly be "all in" for him—committed to become a disciple who was a fully devoted follower of Christ and a servant leader of others.

A.W. Tozer words are so powerful: "Everything is safe which we commit to Him, and nothing is really safe which is not so committed. Our gifts and talents should also be turned over to Him. They should be recognized for what they are, God's loan to us, and should never be considered in any sense our own."[1]

LORD JESUS

There was a movement going around the church at this time about the need to make Christ the "Lord" of your life. The message from the church was, "We know you are saved, but you also need to make another decision to accept Jesus as your Lord." This really messed me up for a couple of years. Many of you will remember it as the "Egypt/Wilderness/Canaan" idea. Once that you become a Christian, you have moved out of Egypt and into the wilderness. Then, you need to go "all in" with Christ so you can live in Canaan.

The only problem with that theological model is it simply is not true. If you doubt what I am saying, just go back and read Hebrews 3-4. You will see that the wilderness really represents lost people who have a "works" mentality of salvation; not Christians who are making a decision to choose Christ's lordship or not.

I want you to understand that once you become a Christian, there is no second decision about lordship. The obvious reason is that Jesus Christ is already Lord. Period.

You can deny that fact or you can yield to that fact, but you cannot change that fact. God the Father felt so strongly about it that Scripture tell us one day every human being who has or ever will live on planet earth will bend the knee and personally confess that supreme truth.

You might be thinking "what is the big deal?" between saying we need to make Jesus our "Lord" compared to saying we need to surrender to his lordship over our lives. The big deal is that we have too low a view of God that leads to too high a view of man. Our pride wants us to think that we are still the one who is able to lead our lives on a daily basis. So, when we make this decision, it's saying that we have done something great for God rather than acknowledging the reality that God is the one who has done something great for us.

Finally, it dawned on me what I was doing. I was in essence saying to God, "Hell rescue, yes. Heaven home, yes. But earth leadership, no thanks. Yes, God, I desperately need your help because I do not want to go to hell, and I know I cannot save myself. I want to live in heaven, but let's talk about this earth thing and see if we can make a deal. I mean, I want you to be a part of my life and I will pray, read my Bible some, and go to church. I definitely want your help when I get in a jam, but just not all the time. I want you to help guide me in some of my decisions, but I think I can handle most of the ones that need to be made."

The most spiritually arrogant thing I have ever done is to tell God that I needed him for eternity but not for the here and now.

This bad theology is still the reason many people live a segmented life—faith has everything to do with Sunday but very little to do with Monday. We trust God for eternity but not for today.

This powerful statement from C.S. Lewis is one we should never forget: "Christianity, if false, is of no importance, and if true, of infinite importance. The only thing it cannot be is moderately important."[2]

AMAZING GRACE

Complete surrender to God means asking him to lead every area of our life. It's a total dependency upon his grace to give us the emotional, physical, and spiritual margin we need to live every day. When we understand his grace, it dramatically impacts our willingness to trust God and let him lead. It is the only way we can consistently meet the demands that come at us every day. If we are not "all in," then we are depending to some degree on ourselves more than we are on him. God promises his presence, peace, and power that we will need for every life situation.

The Christian life was designed by God to be lived with nothing less than 100 percent surrender. Anything less means that, to that degree, you are still trying to maintain control.

Jesus told a story in Luke 7:40-47 that is often overlooked but extremely relevant at this point. The story is being told to a Pharisee who was very upset that Jesus had allowed a very sinful woman to wash his feet.

> And Jesus answering said to him, "Simon, I have something to say to you." And he answered, "Say it, Teacher."
>
> "A certain moneylender had two debtors. One owed five hundred denarii, and the other fifty. When they could not pay, he cancelled the debt of both. Now which of them will love him more?" Simon answered, "The one, I suppose, for whom he cancelled the larger debt." And he said to him, "You have judged rightly." Then turning toward the woman he said to Simon, "Do you see this woman? I entered your house; you gave me no water for my feet, but she has wet my feet with her tears and wiped them with her hair. You gave me no kiss, but from the time I came in she has not ceased to kiss my feet. You did not anoint my head with oil, but she has anointed my feet with ointment. Therefore I tell you, her sins, which are many, are forgiven—for she loved much. But he who is forgiven little, loves little." (Luke 7:40-47)

The Christian life was designed by God to be lived with nothing less than 100 percent surrender. Anything less means that, to that degree, you are still trying to maintain control.

In the story, two people owed a debt—one was a very large sum and the other a small amount—and the lender forgave them both.

> *The amount of your love for God will always be in direct proportion to your gratitude to God. Your gratitude is in direct proportion to your awareness of your need for forgiveness and grace.*

After telling the story, Jesus asked the Pharisee this important question: which debtor in the story do you think is the most grateful to the lender? The Pharisee answered correctly when he said the one who was forgiven the larger debt.

Then, Jesus made this statement about the woman who washed his feet, and, about every one of us:

> *Therefore I tell you, her sins, which are many, are forgiven—for she loved much. But he who is forgiven little, loves little. (Luke 7:47)*

Here is the point of application for every person reading this book: if you see yourself in need of little forgiveness, then you will love little in return. However, if you see yourself the way you really are before God as a hopeless sinner, then you will be grateful and love much.

The amount of your love for God will always be in direct proportion to your gratitude to God. Your gratitude is in direct proportion to your awareness of your need for forgiveness and grace.

Most Christians' view of their personal sin would only have required Jesus to get a slap on the hand rather than a cruel death on the cross as payment. We must clearly see our sinful condition before we will ever appreciate God for what he has done for us. We have a fairly good understanding of the redeeming grace that was necessary for our salvation. However, if you still perceive that you have been forgiven little, then you will give back little love in return.

After redeeming grace, we often still try to comfort ourselves and justify our sin by comparing our sin to those around us. Francis Chan writes, "Lukewarm Christians gauge their morality or goodness by comparing themselves to the secular world. They feel satisfied that while they aren't as hard-core for Jesus as so-and-so, they are nowhere as horrible as the guy down the street."[3]

Refining grace, though, forces you to change the standard and move the bar. You are no longer able to compare yourself with yourself, or even other people, because you now must compare yourself with God. R.C. Sproul makes the point: "Men are never duly touched and impressed with a conviction of their insignificance. Until they have contrasted themselves with the majesty of God."[4]

The word "refine" means to remove all impurities so that something can be brought to a pure state. The moment you become a Christian, by God's grace, you begin a journey to be conformed into the image of Christ.

The God who began that journey has promised he will complete it and get you safely to the other side. We are convicted and chastened, if necessary, for the ongoing sin in our lives because of the love the Father has for his children. He wants you to avoid the pain of sin, and he wants you to represent him well to the world. After all, that is why he left you on earth after he saved you.

Before any Christian will come to the place of complete surrender to God, they must come to a point of personal spiritual brokenness. Jesus calls us into a deeper relationship with him:

> Come to me, all who labor and are heavy laden, and I will
> give you rest. Take my yoke upon you, and learn from me,
> for I am gentle and lowly in heart, and you will find rest for your souls.
> For my yoke is easy, and my burden is light. (Matthew 11:28-30)

Maybe the ultimate tragedy for the Christian is that while Jesus is desperately calling us into a relationship, we, instead, respond with religion. Tozer drives this home: "Similarly, the presence of God is the central fact of Christianity. At the heart of the Christian message is God himself waiting for his redeemed children to push into conscious awareness of his presence."[5]

For some people, spiritual brokenness comes out of a major crisis experience in their lives. It could be the result of an accident, or maybe losing a job, or even a serious health problem. Regardless of how you may get there, spiritual brokenness occurs when your gratitude to God becomes a significantly greater factor in your life than your personal pride and confidence in yourself.

Is it possible, in this life, to get to the place where we totally die to self and to pride? No. However, every Christian can and should reach a point of absolute surrender to God's will for their life.

For me, and for the vast majority of people reading this, we must go deeper than redeeming and refining grace. We must also understand restraining grace before we will fully appreciate all that God has done for us. Restraining grace means that God restrains or limits the total potential impact of sin and evil in our lives as individuals and in the world as a whole. Simply put, we are never as bad as we potentially could be apart from his grace.

We read these horrifying words in Genesis 6:3-5: and the Lord said, "my spirit shall not strive with man forever," then the Lord saw that the wickedness of man was great in the earth, and that every intent of the thoughts of his heart was only evil continually.

The only reason that the world, in general, and people, specifically, are as "good" as they are today is because of the presence of God's restraining grace. When he removes it, all hell breaks loose.

Maybe the ultimate tragedy for the Christian is that while Jesus is desperately calling us into a relationship, we, instead, respond with religion.

> "
>
> *I did not come to a point of spiritual brokenness over an awareness of the sin I had committed, but an awareness of the sin I was capable of committing apart from God's restraining grace in my life.*

I now fully realize the potential depth of depravity I would find myself in apart from the restraining grace of God in my own life. I know painfully well that I am not all that I should be for God. But now, every day of my life, I sincerely and gratefully thank God for the fact that I am not what I could have been. And, by his grace and for his glory, I want to become all that I can be.

I did not come to a point of spiritual brokenness over an awareness of the sin I had committed, but an awareness of the sin I was capable of committing apart from God's restraining grace in my life. Christianity for the 21st century will require people who are broken over their sin and grateful for his daily grace.

Absolute and complete forgiveness received, and unlimited amounts of grace given, means a life of gratitude where radical love is given back in total surrender. Just think about it and let all of the performance-based lies about your relationship with the Father die.

No matter how many times you read your Bible, pray, or go to church, there is nothing you can do to cause the Father to love you any more than he does right now. On the other hand, no matter how many times you fail him, there is nothing you can do to cause him to love you any less than he already does right now. There is no risk involved when the reality of your relationship is unconditionally secure. That is amazing grace.

HOLY TEMPLES

Once I had an understanding of all aspects of grace, and I surrendered to God's leadership of my life, it was time for the next disruptive truth. It is still to this day beyond my ability to comprehend and appreciate the reality that the God who created the universe lives within me. He and I do everything together.

> *Or do you not know that your body is a temple of the Holy Spirit*
> *within you, whom you have from God? You are not your own,*
> *for you were bought with a price. So glorify God in your body.*
> *(1 Corinthians 6:19-20)*

It's one thing to know that God wants me to live with him in heaven one day, but totally another to know that he wants to live within me now. Tozer writes, "The world is perishing for lack of the knowledge of God and the church is famishing for want of His presence. The instant cure of most of our religious ills would be to enter the Presence in spiritual experience, to become suddenly aware that we are in God and that God is in us."[6]

God's eternal plan has always been to be identified with his people, not a place. This relationship started in a garden and will end in a city where we will live with him forever. In this present life, we experience this relationship through his abiding presence living within us. We now have fully moved from a Creator-Creation type of relationship to that of a Father-Son.

Notice the natural progression in our relationship with the Father in Galatians 4: 1-7:

> I mean that the heir, as long as he is a child, is no different
> from a slave, though he is the owner of everything, but he
> is under guardians and managers until the date set by his father.
> In the same way we also, when we were children, were enslaved
> to the elementary principles of the world. But when the fullness
> of time had come, God sent forth his Son, born of woman, born
> under the law, to redeem those who were under the law, so that
> we might receive adoption as sons. And because you are sons,
> God has sent the Spirit of his Son into our hearts, crying,
> "Abba! Father!" So you are no longer a slave, but a son,
> and if a son, then an heir through God.

We were slaves under judgment, but now, through Christ, we are adopted into the family of God as his children. He sends the Holy Spirit to live within us so that we can become sons and daughters, no longer children.

Many Christians get stuck in the child stage of spiritual maturity. They are, in reality, sons and daughters who are tragically still living like slaves. They have a segmented life, with God living in a box instead of within them.

When I preach on the subject of the indwelling presence of God in our lives, I always use this illustration. I begin by talking about the cultural disruption and how ineffective we are at reaching three entire generations. I lean into the whole idea of being relevant to maximize all that the Church Gathered can offer. I intentionally take it to the point of recommending that we serve beer next Sunday in the lobby and show R-rated movie clips to attract a larger crowd. At this point, it is obvious that everyone in the room is becoming uncomfortable. I then make the point that most of us would not want to desecrate this holy place by bringing those things in the church building. Why is it then, some of us will go out this week and order drinks after we attend an R-rated movie, and never give a thought to the fact that we took God with us?

Don't tune me out over debating the social issues I have just raised and miss the point of the illustration. What you need to do is finally and fully come to the realization that you are the holy place, not the church building. If, for whatever reason, it

God's eternal plan has always been to be identified with his people, not a place. This relationship started in a garden and will end in a city where we will live with him forever.

would be wrong for you to do anything on Sunday at the Church Gathered, then it is just as wrong to do it on Monday living in the Church Scattered.

Being God's temple allows us immediate and constant access to the Father and the God of the Universe who wants us to be so intimate with him that we address him as "Abba" or "daddy." If you have a hard time starting any prayer this intimately, then you have not fully realized that yet. Many Christians think it is not reverent or sacred enough, when the reality is that it is the most sacred way you could address him. What is sinful, not sacred, is when we don't fully trust the one who loves us so much. We don't trust because we don't know. We don't know because we are not grateful, and we spend so little time with him.

Tozer speaks the truth again: "Complacency is a deadly foe of all spiritual growth. Acute desire must be present or there will be no manifestation of Christ to His people. He waits to be wanted. Too bad that with many of us He waits so long, so very long, in vain."[7]

We grasp redeeming grace and are no longer afraid of what the Father might do to us through judgment. However, we are still very much afraid of what he might do with us if we went "all in" with his leadership over our life.

Some of the most sacred words ever spoken are found in Christ's prayer to the Father in John 17:

> *But now I am coming to you, and these things I speak in the world, that they may have my joy fulfilled in themselves. I have given them your word, and the world has hated them because they are not of the world, just as I am not of the world. I do not ask that you take them out of the world, but that you keep them from the evil one. They are not of the world, just as I am not of the world. Sanctify them in the truth; your word is truth. As you sent me into the world, so I have sent them into the world. And for their sake I consecrate myself, that they also may be sanctified in truth. I do not ask for these only, but also for those who will believe in me through their word, that they may all be one, just as you, Father, are in me, and I in you, that they also may be in us, so that the world may believe that you have sent me. The glory that you have given me I have given to them, that they may be one even as we are one, I in them and you in me, that they may become perfectly one, so that the world may know that you sent me and loved them even as you loved me. Father, I desire that they also, whom you have given me, may be with me where I am, to see my glory that you have given me because you loved me before the foundation of the world.*

The beauty of these verses lays out the deep desire of our Savior to be with us now and for us to be with him for all eternity. It also shows us the massive responsibility we have as Christians to represent Christ, so that the world may believe that he was sent by God.

This passage always brings me to tears of amazement when I think about how much we are loved. Tozer reminds us all of an extremely important truth: "Worshipers never leave church…We carry our sanctuary with us wherever we go."[8]

This brings me to the major disruptive truth of the chapter and maybe the entire book: we have failed at the Great Commission because we have undervalued the Great Commandment.

> Teacher, which is the great commandment in the Law?"
> And he said to him, "You shall love the Lord your God with all your
> heart and with all your soul and with all your mind. This is the
> great and first commandment. And a second is like it: You shall
> love your neighbor as yourself. On these two commandments
> depend all the Law and the Prophets. (Matthew 22:36-40)

I must guard my heart so that I never lose my first love. Our passion for God drives our compassion for others. But I believe we have confused our priorities for the last fifty years or longer. Again, as with every other truth in this book, it is not so much the right thing versus the wrong thing, but how much priority we give to both. I sit in churches and hear twenty times more about that particular local church and all that makes it important to the community than I hear about Jesus Christ. I need to hear about the glory of God, Jesus Christ, the gospel, mission, calling, kingdom, spiritual maturity, and living every day in the Church Scattered.

Challenging me to be an active member of the local church is not as compelling as totally abandoning my entire life for the gospel. Challenging me to make the secular parts of my life sacred is the most inspiring thing you could ever say.

Discipleship is becoming a fully devoted follower of Christ and a servant leader to others. Ultimately, living our lives for the glory of God needs to get back to the top of the priority list.

I want to circle back to a statement I made earlier in the book: we have so overvalued the Church Gathered over Christ and following him every day in the Church Scattered, that we have reduced the church to a mere commodity in the marketplace of our culture. Whoever has the best facilities, family programming, music, and special events has the competitive advantages that drive attendance.

In corporate life, when an organization does not know what its competitive advantage

This brings me to the major disruptive truth of the chapter and maybe the entire book: we have failed at the Great Commission because we have undervalued the Great Commandment.

is, they will take something of lower value and move it to the top. As we face the challenge of reaching these three generations, we better have Jesus Christ at the top of our messaging, not just the church or Christianity. Again, the church is not the hope of the world—Christ is. Your security and significance in this life are not your career, marriage, or children—Christ is.

THE PREEMINENCE OF CHRIST

> *He is the image of the invisible God, the firstborn of all creation. For by him all things were created, in heaven and on earth, visible and invisible, whether thrones or dominions or rulers or authorities—all things were created through him and for him. And he is before all things, and in him all things hold together. And he is the head of the body, the church. He is the beginning, the firstborn from the dead, that in everything he might be preeminent. For in him all the fullness of God was pleased to dwell, and through him to reconcile to himself all things, whether on earth or in heaven, making peace by the blood of his cross. (Colossians 1:15-20)*

Tozer's prayer is very fitting at the point: "Please root from my heart all those things which I have cherished so long and which have become a very part of my living self, so that You may enter and dwell there without a rival."[9]

THE PROCESS

The process is when God continues to work in our lives in such a way that he exposes our sin to us so that we can change. He also is preparing us for our mission of loving our neighbors as ourselves.

> *And I am sure of this, that he who began a good work in you will bring it to completion at the day of Jesus Christ. (Philippians 1:6)*

The goal now is not salvation, but Christlikeness. He wants everyone to be able to see Christ in us so they can be drawn to knowing him. The Father is a loving parent who wants what is best for his children. He must first work in us before he can work through us to impact others.

The two major needs that we as human beings are searching for in life are security and significance. Security is the understanding that I am unconditionally loved, and significance means that my life has value and meaning.

God created us this way so there would be a void in our lives that only he could meet. Most of the time we are searching to have these needs met in all of the wrong places. We try to find unconditional love in human relationships that inevitably fail us to some degree and cause pain. For many Christians, we believe that if we can just marry the right person, then all of our needs will be met. We are looking for someone to love us unconditionally and meet our emotional needs. It doesn't take long for us to realize that the other person is just as broken as we are. Then, we attempt to "fix" them, which causes even more pain.

Although we claim that we've given our lives to Christ, we struggle to put him first on our priority list, so the cycle continues.

For many of us, since we can't seem to have our needs met in our relationships, we then turn to the culture that tells us all of our needs will be met in the success of our career. We will definitely find more security and significance there than in our marriages, we tell ourselves. And, after all, we have to provide for our families, so career seems to be the next best thing to move up to the top spot on our priority list.

At some point, our career will start to break down after missing that promotion or working for a toxic boss, and we're at a loss once again. So, how about moving our children to the top of the list? This works well for about the first ten years of their childhood. We feel extremely significant and affirmed because of all the love and care they need from us. But, here again, our children soon become teenagers, and we all know what that means.

Since nothing is really stable at work anymore, and the children are about to launch, how about moving church up the top of the list? That is clearly giving more priority to faith and God, so it has to be the answer. Surely, God will notice the effort and reward us accordingly. Sadly, we can get extremely active in the church and use our service to hide the real problems.

Here again, although all of these are "good" things and can give us some degree of security and significance, they also, in the end, leave us desperately wanting more.

All human relationships are important, and we should want to succeed at building healthy ones. However, the major truth we are missing is, we can never look to other people or things to give us what only God can provide.

When our relationship with God is first and his mission for our life is the ultimate measure of our success, then all other relationships and endeavors play a secondary role and become complementary and not primary.

Great careers, marriages, children, and friends are intended to be human expressions of the divine reality. They can offer some degree of security and significance, but they should never be the number one priority in our life.

As Corrie ten Boom said, "Every experience God gives us, every person He puts in

The two major needs that we as human beings are searching for in life are security and significance. Security is the understanding that I am unconditionally loved, and significance means that my life has value and meaning.

our lives, is the perfect preparation for a future that only He can see."[10]

The foundational truth about the process is that God has been on a mission from before you were even born. He is using every person and every experience in your life to draw you into a closer relationship with him.

I have counseled hundreds of married couples, and I always hear the same story. Each person thinks the other person is the real problem, and, if they would change, everything in the marriage would be great. The shock on their faces and the silence in the room comes when I share more about the process. I tell them that God is actually using their spouse to reveal things to them about themselves they would not learn any other way. The same thing is true about your career failures, problem children, failing health, unfaithful friends, and bad church experiences.

The second truth I want you to see about the process is, what God wants you to see about yourself is not related to the relationship or issues, but directly to your relationship with him.

Most of us can muster up an apology when we have wronged or hurt someone. The step we miss as Christians is to ask for God's forgiveness first because our sin is ultimately against him. We tend to ask for mercy from him yet demand justice for others. This lack of gratitude for his grace grieves him. We are hurt more than he is when we sin, but when you are in a relationship, both matter.

There is one more hard truth here that we must understand. When we put someone or something in the place where only God should be, the resulting pain is primarily on us. We never should have placed the expectation on them to be the primary source of our security and significance in the first place. It was our spiritual immaturity that placed them there.

The core problem lies in having too high a view of man and too low a view of God. He alone, by the nature of who he is, must be our number one priority. Then, when pain, failure, and rejection inevitably come in this life, they can be measured against the grace and peace that only God can give. The assurance that he will never leave us and that nothing can separate us from his love gives us the courage to risk living life on mission to the fullest.

In the end, he is more than enough.

What then shall we say to these things? If God is for us, who can be against us? He who did not spare his own Son but gave him up for us all, how will he not also with him graciously give us all things? Who shall bring any charge against God's elect? It is God who justifies. Who is to condemn? Christ Jesus is the one who died—more than that,

*who was raised—who is at the right hand of God, who indeed is
interceding for us. Who shall separate us from the love of Christ?
Shall tribulation, or distress, or persecution, or famine, or nakedness,
or danger, or sword? As it is written, "For your sake we are being killed
all the day long; we are regarded as sheep to be slaughtered."
No, in all these things we are more than conquerorsthrough him
who loved us. For I am sure that neither death nor life, nor angels
nor rulers, nor things present nor things to come, nor powers,
nor height nor depth, nor anything else in all creation,
will be able to separate us from the love of God in Christ
Jesus our Lord. (Romans 8:31-39)*

GOOD SAMARITAN

This brings us to the second part of the Great Commandment, which is to love our neighbor as ourselves. Our neighbor should be seen as anyone God divinely brings into our lives who we can move one step closer to Christ. They can be our literal neighbors down the street. This one is so important in this culture because being someone's neighbor creates more openness to build trust than any other type of relationship. This also includes our co-workers, friends, clients, suppliers, real estate agents, grocery store clerks, waiters, car repair employees, gym warriors, and coffee shop baristas. You are their best chance to find God and that should give you more significance than being the CEO of Amazon.

There is one incredible and familiar passage that brings all of this together:

*But he, desiring to justify himself, said to Jesus, "And who is
my neighbor?" Jesus replied, "A man was going down from Jerusalem
to Jericho, and he fell among robbers, who stripped him and beat
him and departed, leaving him half dead. Now by chance a
priest was going down that road, and when he saw him he passed
by on the other side. So likewise a Levite, when he came to the
place and saw him, passed by on the other side. But a Samaritan,
as he journeyed, came to where he was, and when he saw him,
he had compassion. He went to him and bound up his wounds,
pouring on oil and wine. Then he set him on his own animal
and brought him to an inn and took care of him. And the next
day he took out two denarii and gave them to the innkeeper, saying,
'Take care of him, and whatever more you spend, I will repay you
when I come back.' Which of these three, do you think, proved to be
a neighbor to the man who fell among the robbers?" He said,
"The one who showed him mercy." And Jesus said to him,
"You go, and do likewise." (Luke 10:29-37)*

The foundational truth about the process is that God has been on a mission from before you were even born. He is using every person and every experience in your life to draw you into a closer relationship with him.

Let's start with the person in the ditch. That represents all of us before Christ came to rescue, redeem, and restore us. Fellow Christians, until we understand the restraining grace of God in our life, we will always love little. We will see ourselves as the passers-by in the story. This is the reason why we turn away. You will never stop to help someone in the ditch until you first see yourself as having lived there, too. Then, you finally begin to comprehend that God rescued you from the ditch just like the Samaritan in the parable. You were the one that he left the ninety-nine to find. He bound up your wounds, took you to a healing place, and paid for the entire cost of your care for eternity.

Our passion for others, and for completing our mission, is driven solely by our passion for God. Our love for others will flow out of our love for him. The gratitude we have for Christ cannot be expressed in any other way than in our response of, "Here am I! Send me."

Checking the box of church attendance and program participation is no longer acceptable. The words of Richard Stearns are powerful: "Belief is not enough. Worship is not enough. Personal morality is not enough. Christian community is not enough. When we have committed ourselves to following Christ, we are also committed to living our lives in such a way that a watching world would catch a glimpse of God's character—His love, justice, and mercy—through our words, actions and behavior."[11]

Now, with a clear view of ourselves and of God, we want to represent Jesus to everyone. It begins the process of merging both the sacred and secular parts of our lives.

STORYTELLERS

Our role in this mission is to first allow the Father to do his deep work in us. Then, we are finally ready for him to work through us. When he does, we now will give him all the glory.

Probably one of the best-known passages about our responsibility in the mission is in the first chapter of the Book of Acts:

> *But you will receive power when the Holy Spirit has come upon you, and you will be my witnesses in Jerusalem and in all Judea and Samaria, and to the end of the earth. (Acts 1:8)*

A witness is someone who simply shares with others what he or she has seen and heard. It's your gospel story and takes less than thirty minutes to write down. It includes your life before Christ, how you came to know Christ as Lord, and how he is living in your life today. It is probably not the conversation you lead with, but it's the one you have ready to share when the opportunity is right. All of that depends on where the person is on their receptivity scale.

This does not require a seminary degree or evangelism training. It does require an intentional investment in making spiritual deposits in another person's life. You actually will pray more for them than you will talk to them.

AMBASSADORS

The following passage takes our responsibility to represent Christ to the world to an entirely different level. It clearly shows the divine partnership of how God is working directly through us to draw people to himself:

> ...that is, in Christ God was reconciling the world to himself, not counting their trespasses against them, and entrusting to us the message of reconciliation. Therefore, we are ambassadors for Christ, God making his appeal through us. We implore you on behalf of Christ, be reconciled to God. For our sake he made him to be sin who knew no sin, so that in him we might become the righteousness of God.
> (2 Corinthians 5:19-21)

So, our significance comes from representing God to the world as his ambassador. In comparison, the president of the United States cannot touch this degree of importance.

The astounding good news of the gospel is this: Christ who knew no sin became sin for us so that we might become the forgiven children of God. The urgency of our mission cannot be missed; we implore or urge others to consider the claims of Jesus Christ—he is God, and our only way to heaven is through faith in his death on the cross.

LEADERS

Every individual is the leader of his or her own life. The decisions we make every day let people know about our priorities and passion. Most of us go to work and, again, because of the sheer time invested there, we must treat this as our greatest public platform for ministry.

Although the context of these next passages may have been the first century, the truth has never been more relevant:

> Bondservants, obey in everything those who are your earthly masters, not by way of eye-service, as people-pleasers, but with sincerity of heart, fearing the Lord. Whatever you do, work heartily, as for the Lord and not for men, knowing that from the Lord you will receive the inheritance as your reward. You are serving the Lord Christ. (Colossians 3:22-24)

> *The urgency of our mission cannot be missed; we implore or urge others to consider the claims of Jesus Christ—he is God, and our only way to heaven is through faith in his death on the cross.*

Walk in wisdom toward outsiders, making the best use of the time. Let your speech always be gracious, seasoned with salt, so that you may know how you ought to answer each person. (Colossians 4:5-6)

One of the first major disruptive truths in this book is that God is calling every Christian to be a disciple and to leverage their work as part of God's sacred mission for their life. The merging of faith and work must be done so that we can leverage our leadership influence to impact people every single day.

For example, when people see you being mistreated at work, and that you respond to that mistreatment with the fruit of the spirit, it is nothing less than supernatural.

But even if you should suffer for righteousness' sake, you will be blessed. Have no fear of them, nor be troubled, but in your hearts honor Christ the Lord as holy, always being prepared to make a defense to anyone who asks you for a reason for the hope that is in you; yet do it with gentleness and respect, having a good conscience, so that, when you are slandered, those who revile your good behavior in Christ may be put to shame. (1 Peter 3:14-16)

When you love your enemies and are kind to those who spitefully use you for their own gain, then you've brought your worship to work. When the yoke is on, then Christ promises rest in our work because he is working there with us toward the ultimate bottom line. What does it profit a person if they indeed gain the whole world and are lost for eternity?

BROKEN VESSELS

This role speaks to the absolute necessity for spiritual brokenness in our lives. Until we completely die to any performance-based relationship with the Father, our motivation will be, to some degree, for ourselves. The result is, as in the parable, we will keep walking by on the other side of the road to avoid those in the ditch.

For God, who said, "Let light shine out of darkness," has shone in our hearts to give the light of the knowledge of the glory of God in the face of Jesus Christ. But we have this treasure in jars of clay, to show that the surpassing power belongs to God and not to us. We are afflicted in every way, but not crushed; perplexed, but not driven to despair; persecuted, but not forsaken; struck down, but not destroyed; always carrying in the body the death of Jesus, so that the life of Jesus may also be manifested in our bodies. (2 Corinthians 4:6-10)

We must understand that if the vessel is not broken, then the grace cannot leak out to move others toward Christ. Spiritual brokenness represents the heart of a disciple who gladly surrenders to his leader because he trusts him completely. This part of the process is taking place every day with every person we interact with regardless of where it is. Because Christ lives within us, we can turn any grocery store into a holy place.

> But thanks be to God, who in Christ always leads us in triumphal procession, and through us spreads the fragrance of the knowledge of him everywhere. For we are the aroma of Christ to God among those who are being saved and among those who are perishing, to one a fragrance from death to death, to the other a fragrance from life to life. Who is sufficient for these things? (2 Corinthians 2:14-16)

Small acts of kindness become cups of cold water for someone who does not know Christ. On my walk every morning, I intentionally stop and pick up the paper in one of my neighbors' yards and put it on the porch. Recently, one of my neighbors asked me if I was the one helping with his paper. I told him yes, and he responded "thanks" and quickly rolled up the window. Last week, he opened the front door just as I was putting the paper on his porch. This encounter was completely different than the first. He greeted me with a warm smile, handshake, and kind words. I am constantly praying for him to come to know Christ.

There is an absolute tension in the Great Commission between reaching the lost and maturing them in the faith. We must do both to fulfill the mandate of making disciples. My conviction is that, for the majority of Christians, the reason they are not reaching lost people is because they have not become disciples themselves. We have reduced discipleship to church attendance rather than following Christ.

Francis Chan puts it this way: "People who are obsessed with God have an intimate relationship with Him. They are nourished by God's Word throughout the day because they know that forty minutes on Sunday is not enough to sustain them for the whole week, especially when they will encounter so many distractions and alternative messages."[12]

I also have another absolute conviction that Christian disciples who are former "ditch dwellers" will not pass by those on the side of the road needing help. I believe it is impossible to love little when you have been passionately loved so much.

David Platt pours out his heart in response to the heart of God: "For the sake of a billion people today who have yet to even hear the gospel, I want to risk it all. For the sake of 26,000 children who will die today of starvation or a preventable disease, I

When you love your enemies and are kind to those who spitefully use you for their own gain, then you've brought your worship to work.

want to risk it all. For the sake of an increasingly marginalized and relatively ineffective church in our culture, I want to risk it all. For the sake of my life, my family and the people who surround me, I want to risk it all."[13]

Actually, when you are completely secure and significant in the One who holds you in the grip of his grace, there is no risk at all.

DISRUPTIVE TRUTHS

The Great Commandment must be significantly prioritized over the Great Commission.

God is conforming us into the image of Christ for our good and his glory.

Our compassion for others is a direct result of our passion for God.

Jesus Christ is Lord and, therefore, should be followed in total surrender.

We are never as bad as we could be apart from God's restraining grace in our lives.

We are the holy place of God, and we do everything together.

Our calling and mission are to know Christ and make him known.

Chapter Five: Church Gathered

The first question I am asked when people hear the vision for prioritizing the Church Scattered is "Do you think this will hurt the Church Gathered?" My answer is that not only do I think it will help; it may rescue it from becoming irrelevant to unbelievers.

Is there some risk that if we go too far in changing our methods that we could compromise our beliefs? No. It's our message that is sacred, not our methods. The even greater risk is to change nothing and continue to experience the downward cycle of three lost generations.

I am not going to spend any more time making the case for the conviction I have that the church is in a state of disruption. If you don't agree with my conclusions in the first three chapters, then the rest of the book will probably be a waste. I am also not going to develop an entire theological argument for the role of the Church Gathered in accomplishing the mission of God. It should speak loudly to you that I have called this movement the *Church* Scattered: Christianity for 21st century. I could have called it *Missionaries* Scattered, *Disciples* Scattered, *Christians* Scattered or any other para-church cool ministry name like *"Glocal"* Ministries. However, with all my heart and soul, I believe that everything I am recommending is within the mission of the church.

It's our message that is sacred, not our methods.

We gather together to worship our glorious God as a body of believers united in our kingdom mission. We also worship through attendance, prayer, music, message, baptism, communion, and giving. We experience community as we serve one another through the ministry of our spiritual gifts. We cry with those who are hurting and give them a hug. We also rejoice with those who are experiencing blessings.

Yes, the discipline of showing up still matters because others are counting on you for encouragement and accountability:

> Let us hold fast the confession of our hope without wavering,
> for he who promised is faithful. And let us consider how to stir up one
> another to love and good works, not neglecting to meet together,
> as is the habit of some, but encouraging one another, and all the
> more as you see the Day drawing near. (Hebrews 10:23-25)

While there are going to be opportunities to leverage technology to reach and equip people in becoming disciples, I cannot touch you with a tweet, text message, on Facebook Live, or if you are streaming the church service at home. As you can

> *Through Christian community, we can help others find their calling and mission by showing them how to merge the secular and sacred into one abundant life.*

see, I believe the Church Gathered is crucial to cultivating healthy community.

The whole world is longing for relational community and that is one of the things the church can do better than anyone else. Remember, everyone is searching for security and significance in their life. We are the only organization that knows the answer to the world's deepest needs, and when we introduce them to Jesus Christ, everything can change. Through Christian community, we can help others find their calling and mission by showing them how to merge the secular and sacred into one abundant life.

I want to spend the rest of this chapter talking solutions more than problems. This section is based on my years of both sitting in the pew and standing behind a pulpit.

I admit that some of my recommendations may be flawed, and I welcome input from others. I also freely admit that the personal pain that I have experienced influences some of my conclusions. I trust the Holy Spirit to speak to you what he wants you to hear. Then, it will be up to you to do whatever he tells you to do.

CHURCH SIZE

Most of us know the data that reports up to 85 percent of all churches in North America average under 150 people in attendance each Sunday. I want to make some recommendations for the churches in this category that probably will never grow beyond that number.

Some of the churches are in this category because they are new church plants or multi-site campuses, and, therefore, have the potential to grow beyond 500. If that is your category, then all of the things I will say later will clearly apply to the strategy you develop.

However, most of the churches in this smaller category are in rural areas and are dealing with the urban flight that is impacting their communities. I do believe that any church should seek to grow in number as long as there are lost people within your reach.

Two disruptive changes are occurring that can help small churches. First, the generations that we as the church are trying to reach place a higher value on community than programming and special events.

Please remember, before you will love people regardless of their background, you will have to move the Great Commandment to the top of the priority list. If you are not willing to do that, then you might as well give away the property or sell it and give the money to missions.

Secondly, when you change the scorecard for smaller churches, they immediately become effective again. No matter how small your church may be, that should never be an excuse for not fulfilling the Great Commission. You must do everything you can to reach and equip disciples. However, I don't find a requirement anywhere in the New Testament that these disciples must also become members of your church. Many churches lose their passion and vision because it has been years since any young couples have walked in their door. If that's you, don't be discouraged. All that means is that it's time for you to walk in theirs.

There is no excuse today for any church to not live out the gospel in a nearby city ministry or, for that matter, anywhere else in the world. Partner with other churches with different cultures and help them reach people for Christ. Then, they can assimilate them into their churches, putting you back in the harvest again.

While pastoring a smaller church, I quickly realized that the potential for reaching people in the local area was limited. No one had come to faith in Christ and been baptized in a long time. So, we planned two mission trips to get back into the harvest. We took one trip and worked with an existing church in more of a pioneer area. The results were encouraging and the people who went had gospel stories to share with the church on our return. The next step was to partner with mission organizations and take seven people, including teenagers, on an international trip to a remote town in Venezuela. The life change was dramatic and the stories about what God was doing around the world were powerful for all to hear.

The institutional culture that won't allow new disciples who don't become members of your church to be included in your annual report, is hurting the church. It's as if this ministry does not count as success for the local church.

Also, technology today allows the smaller church to participate in the absolute best preaching, teaching, and equipping that is available to any larger church. Smaller churches can have an advantage if they will get back into the harvest and give people access to the best development possible. This will require a new level of leadership training for small church pastors. Shepherds can now become ranchers, so to speak, by leveraging the Church Scattered for reaching people.

CHURCH LEADERSHIP

A painful reality is that more problems occur in churches because of poor leadership than any theological controversy. This leadership crisis starts at the top and then trickles down to the members.

Again, I believe that seminaries should devote a full third of their training to leadership development and another third to cross-cultural missions. Denominational agencies will also need to help in filling this void or they risk becoming irrelevant.

Smaller churches can have an advantage if they will get back into the harvest and give people access to the best development possible.

This leadership development crisis is not unique to the church. Every major corporation where I do executive coaching struggles with all of these same issues. Older industrial age leaders use directive positional authority more than collaboration. They, in reality, are insecure and assume that if they delegate and empower other people, they have diminished their own role.

Many others will avoid conflict at all cost and let the organization suffer rather than deal with the problem. This, in the end, is primarily a character problem revealing that they care more about their individual success than the development of others.

You can find toxic, dominant, ego-driven leaders on the one extreme and others who are people-pleasers and unwilling to tell anyone "no."

I have been in key leadership positions in both the corporate world and non-profit organizations. Beyond any doubt, leading in the non-profit culture is the most difficult.

The seminary training that I received back in the 1980s was perfect for a single staff pastor trying to shepherd 100 people. If this seminary model has not changed, it is a disaster for any leader in a context beyond 300.

I have combined my corporate and church leadership experience to put this cultural context into perspective. Senior church leaders are trying to lead a group of people who are also their customers, financial investors, and volunteer work force. No corporate leader has faced that challenge and that reality should give them a greater appreciation for their church staff leaders. On the other hand, church leaders have the greatest brand in the history of the world to meet the greatest need known to man.

In addition to that challenge, church leaders are also managing a staff team that likely was hired because they were great at doing ministry. When the student ministry is running less than fifty, the staff member excels. When the student ministry grows to beyond 150, they start to crash. The issue isn't that they are not called and gifted to work in the church, but that they have not received the proper training to empower other leaders.

Student ministry beyond 200 kids requires the person in charge to become a leader of volunteer church leaders who actually do the ministry. Far too many staff members are hired to do the work instead of partnering with church members to lead the work. The biblical mandate for church leaders is to equip others to do the ministry.

If church members hire staff to do the ministry, and the staff is either unable or unwilling to surrender the ministry, then it is easy to understand why the church is suffering from dramatic disruption and decline.

The ultimate expression of this massive failure is the current clergy-laity paradigm. This leads to the "professionals" hearing from God and the members following. Or, the members taking leadership responsibility and hiring the staff to do the work. Both of these extremes are clearly unbiblical.

Because church staff have not been developed as leaders, they hold on tightly to doing the ministry because they fear losing their jobs. On the other extreme, the laity have gladly outsourced the demands of individual discipleship to the staff.

David Platt is totally on point here: "In this process we have unnecessarily and unbiblically drawn a line of distinction, assigning the obligations of Christianity to a few while keeping the privileges of Christianity for us all."[1]

These institutional distinctions should not exist when it comes to the responsibilities of every Christian disciple. We are all called to ministry—different gifts and roles but the same mission. The clergy-laity walls need to be torn down and replaced with a shared culture that does not minimize the staff but elevates the daily role of Christians.

If we don't fix this dysfunctional and unbiblical culture, we have no hope of empowering members to live out their faith in the Church Scattered. We will continue to use them as workers who support the programs of the institution run by the church professionals.

It seems that many churches hit a wall when they reach the 500 average attendance mark. By that time, if the right leaders are not in place from top to bottom, then growth slows or stops, leaving everyone wondering why.

Some staff members have the character and competency to be coached and can become great leaders. Others, for many reasons, cannot. In those cases, church leaders, especially executive staff, must help them in moving on for their sake and that of the church.

The lack of spiritual maturity among all levels of church leadership will cause many churches to crash at this point. We must make sure that all church leaders are competent to meet the current challenges. If you can get beyond this emotional struggle and trust the Holy Spirit, then great things can begin to happen.

Another critical issue is making sure you have the right organizational leadership culture in place. When I coach with corporate groups, this is what I am looking for:

1. How are priorities set?
2. How are decisions made?
3. How is information communicated?
4. How are results measured?

The clergy-laity walls need to be torn down and replaced with a shared culture that does not minimize the staff but elevates the daily role of Christians.

My preference in both church and corporate culture is to have a shared leadership culture. This means that no one person will decide how to answer all four of those questions.

Remember, great leaders today don't have all the answers, but they do know how to ask the right questions. How this dynamic plays out with the senior church leader is critical.

Today, some still prefer the Moses model—they want their senior leader to get alone with God and come back and tell them what he said. I believe the primary reason for this is that they are afraid to get alone with God and ask for themselves.

I prefer the "first among equals" approach. Regardless of whether your culture uses senior staff leaders or elders/deacons, the senior leader should be given the opportunity to be heard with deference. Leadership demands proactive action and accountability for results. That senior leader must be both humble and courageous. If your senior leader cannot do this, please don't change your culture to compensate—change the person.

Lead pastors, please hear my heart on all of what I am saying about your role in this crisis. It is not primarily your fault, but you must step up and realize that it is your primary responsibility to fix it.

I also do not like the third option of "one among equals." If the senior leader has only an equal voice and vote, then you are leading by simple majority and not biblical priority.

This shared leadership culture should be driven down throughout the congregation. There will be executive leadership teams that can help to communicate strategic priorities and evaluate the effectiveness of results. Ministry teams composed of both staff and lay leaders can help develop and then execute ministry plans. These are the people on the front lines and their voices must be heard.

The first question I always asked when a new ministry strategy was being planned was "who are the church members who can lead this?" Remember, you have people who are capable of planning a strategy to reach Hong Kong who are standing in the lobby handing out bulletins.

If you have a congregational form of church government, then in some critical situations the entire church membership can be involved in major decisions. These meetings allow for vision casting, storytelling, and transparency where appropriate and great opportunities for feedback.

Every executive church leadership team should make sure that every key leader and team have specific measurable goals to accomplish, with quarterly reviews. It is absolutely impossible to maintain alignment without knowing what is happening and why.

At the top of this priority list should be leadership development that includes cross-cultural missions strategy. (Just be sure you are not getting a modified version of the seminary model that more aligns with ministry in Berea than Athens.)

There is absolutely no reason that large church teams could not benefit from the "best practices" that corporate leaders receive every year. Great material exists on teamwork, meeting effectiveness, vision casting, strategic planning, productivity, financial management, and the critical areas of hiring and firing. You, as a church leader, could go through this yourself or hire someone to help with the training. If you simply asked, you probably have a corporate leader who would be glad to give of their time to facilitate.

Just think, the corporate men and women in your membership can bring world-class leadership development to your staff. That mindset, my friends, is a long way from the "how do we get more workers for Sunday service" thinking of churches today.

DISCIPLESHIP PROCESS

Since we are in the business of making disciples, we must do whatever it takes to be successful. There must be an intentional process in place that requires assessment, alignment, commitment to next steps, and ongoing evaluation.

In my opinion, it is absolutely necessary to clearly communicate your expectations on discipleship in a required membership class. If you are developing this membership covenant approach in an existing church, it is worth taking the entire church through the process in a Sunday morning sermon series.

Here is a great example of a covenant developed with a team I have used in multiple churches:

"Having received Christ as my Lord and Savior, and having been baptized by immersion, and being in agreement with the churches statement of beliefs, purpose, strategy, and core values, I now feel led by the Holy Spirit to unite with this church family. In doing so, I commit myself to God and to the other members to do the following:

1.) I will submit myself to the authority of the Scriptures as the final arbiter in all issues. (Psalm 119; 2 Timothy 3:14-17; 2 Peter 1:19-21)

2.) I will commit to assume a personal responsibility for my own spiritual growth

> *There must be an intentional process in place that requires assessment, alignment, commitment to next steps, and ongoing evaluation.*

and that of my family. In making this commitment, I will take the following personal actions in my own life (I John 2:12-14; 1 Peter 2:2; Deut. 6:4-9):

a.) I will complete a personal spiritual evaluation tool with my coach that will determine the next steps to help me move in my spiritual journey.

b.) I will identify a person who will be a relational accountability partner to me. This person could come from a class, group, team, or a spiritual coach provided by the church, or someone in my life who is currently serving in this role.

c.) I will participate throughout the year in the next steps that have been identified to help me grow spiritually and reevaluate with my accountability partner once a year to determine my progress and set new goals for the next year.

3.) I will regularly participate in the life of the church by attending weekly services, engaging in biblical community, inviting and welcoming guests, and serving within and outside the church. (Acts 2:42-47; Hebrews 10:22-25; Titus 3:14)

4.) I will steward the resources God has given me, including time, talents, spiritual gifts, and finances. This includes regular financial giving to the ministry of the church. (Deut. 14:23; Matt. 25:14-30; Romans 12:1-2; 2 Cor. 8-9; 1 Peter 4:10-11)

5.) By God's grace and through the power of the Holy Spirit, I will seek to walk in holiness in all areas of my life, as an act of worship to Jesus Christ. I will merge the secular and sacred parts of my life to live on mission every day. (Phil 1:27; 1 Peter 1:13-16; 4:1-3)

6.) I will submit to the leadership of the elders and other appointed leaders and will be diligent to strive for unity and peace within the church. (Eph. 4:1-3; Hebrews 13:17; 1 Peter 5:5)

One critical comment at this point: if you are willing to lead with this degree of biblical intentionality, it is imperative that the staff leaders are doing all of this in their individual lives and families. The major disruptive truth in this covenant is found in Section 2 of the listed responsibilities. Many staff leaders live with no spiritual growth because they are too busy spending all of their time doing ministry. Do all that you can to train them to be leaders and challenge them to be disciples. However, if they are either unwilling or unable to do both, then, again, it is probably time for them to go.

Another point to make is, this type of purpose and accountability is exactly what these three generations we are trying to reach are looking for in a church. Sure, some people will read that covenant and walk. Others, though, will totally buy in and, with the integration of their faith and work, change the world.

Gabe Lyons is making the point of full faith integration: "Christians seeing themselves as called to merge the sacred and the secular to live on mission for Christ. The churches that recognize that this move is underway find themselves in the middle of what could be the greatest transformation in how Christians have consistently engaged culture in a century."[2]

Fortunately, there are many gifted people who are developing a lot of discipleship models and content. Rick Warren's baseball diamond and concentric circles of taking people through an intentional discipleship process is still excellent material.

The most exhaustive model that I have used in several churches started with the research documented in the book *Move* by Greg Hawkins. This approach has been expanded now under the Reveal approach.[3] The core idea is to have all of your members take an assessment that will place them in one of four stages of spiritual growth:

Exploring Christ: Have a basic belief in God, but they are unsure about Christ and his role in their lives.

Growing in Christ: Have a personal relationship with Christ. They've made a commitment to trust him with their soul's salvation and for eternity, but they are just beginning to learn what it means and what it takes to develop a relationship with him.

Close to Christ: Depend on Christ every day. They see Christ as someone who assists them in life. On a daily basis, they turn to him for help and guidance for the issues they face.

Christ-Centered: Would identify their relationship with Christ as the most important relationship in their entire lives.[4]

If your church is healthy, you should, over time, have people in all four of these categories. However, the priority of the Great Commandment means that if you want lots of "Exploring Christ" people in your church, then produce lots of "Christ-Centered" disciples.

Remember, one of the foundational leadership truths is this: if you don't measure it, then it really does not matter. To say that spiritual maturity cannot be measured in the Church Scattered is absurd and an abrogation of leadership responsibility. The value of assessment is critical in working with lost people to determine where they are on their receptivity scale. The same must be said for every person who is attending your church.

The old programming model that basically said "let's ask everyone to come to everything" was a disaster. For example, personally, I don't need to be sitting in a basic marriage conference; I should be at home unconditionally loving my wife and encouraging my children.

Every church should have a well-defined discipleship process that, once someone knows where they are spiritually, their appropriate next steps can be determined. Next steps have at least three key components that are based on a person's spiritual growth and current stage of life:[5]

1) Priority Needs
2) Best Practice Content
3) Appropriate Platform for Delivery

For example, I am a young married adult without children in the "Growing in Christ" category. I have a high priority for biblical stewardship training to lead my family well. For the sake of illustration, let's say Financial Peace University is the best practice content and the best platform to deliver would be a 12-week class that meets on Sunday morning. Does everyone in the worship service need this content and is that the best platform for delivery? It could be done, but probably not effectively. The critical leadership issue here is alignment.

How about addiction recovery or parenting teenagers? Are these great ideas for a sermon series? The content is an extremely high priority, but the platform does not fit most of the people in the room.

I hope by now you are getting my point. An effective intentional discipleship process must define every major stage of life with its appropriate spiritual maturity level. Then, based on those two variables, the next step is to determine the best practice content and the most effective platform to use for delivery. If you are allowing a group of senior adults to take a class on how to study their Bibles, your church has a major problem. If you are putting "Exploring Christ" millennials in a small group that is going to use inductive Bible study to go through the Book of Romans, your church has a major problem.

According to the *Move* research, as people grow spiritually, they move from one stage to the next.[6]

Movement 1: from "Exploring Christ" to "Growing in Christ"

Movement 1 is all about Christian basics. Developing a firm foundation of spiritual beliefs and attitudes is critical during this trust-building phase. The impact of church activities on spiritual growth is most significant in this movement.

Movement 2: from "Growing in Christ" to "Close to Christ"

In Movement 2, people decide that their relationship with Jesus is personal to them. It hinges on developing a routine of personal spiritual practices that make space and time for a growing intimacy with Christ.

Movement 3: from "Close to Christ" to "Christ-Centered"

In Movement 3, believers replace secular self-centeredness with Christlike self-sacrifice. They pour out their increasing love for Jesus through spiritual outreach activities, especially evangelism.

All of this confirmed for me another great leadership principle: you need to have your best leaders working on your greatest opportunities. The reality is that most of these opportunities today live in the Church Scattered.

Without this degree of intentionality, we will be doing lots of preaching, teaching, and training but none of it will be effectively aligned with what each person needs next in their spiritual journey. Activity does not equal accomplishment and busy is not better.

Spreadsheets should be built that track all of these variables and their relationship to each other. Every sermon series, small group study, class content, special event, and all website posts should be aligned for maximum discipleship effectiveness.

Church members go to work and live with this degree of intentionality and accountability every day. Without alignment, there can be no sustainable competitive advantage that produces a profit. Without a profit, there can be no jobs.

Church leaders, this is now your role in the discipleship process. Your first priority, like every other Christian in the church, is to live out the Great Commandment. You must keep Christ as your first love and intentionally build relationships with lost people.

Most staff members are worried about what they will do if the church gives away the ministry. What I say to them is this: become a competent leader who owns your area of ministry expertise. First, define the priority needs of your people and recommend both the best practice content and appropriate platform for delivery. It will never be effective to take the easy way out and give everyone access to "Right Now Media" and think that the problem is solved. You are equipping church members to do the work of the ministry in every area of their life, not just on Sunday morning. This radical leadership transition of roles must happen.

You need to have your best leaders working on your greatest opportunities. The reality is that most of these opportunities today live in the Church Scattered.

> *You must live it out to the point that you have stories to tell about how God is working in your own life.*

You cannot pass on to them what you have read in a book and think that will be effective. You must live it out to the point that you have stories to tell about how God is working in your own life.

How effective do you really think you are when you are challenging others to develop intentional relationships with lost people and you have none of your own? We should thank these three generations for demanding authenticity from their leaders and not just hype.

DISCIPLESHIP STRATEGY

Here is a detailed strategy for all that I have challenged you with:

Biblical Definition of Success — Priority must be on spiritual maturity and not just attendance. Every member must assume the personal responsibility to become a fully devoted follower of Christ.

Establish Comprehensive Process — Starting from birth throughout every stage of life. It is critical for the new member process to lay the foundation for this individualized journey.

Communicate Clear Model — Develop a tool that shows progressive spiritual formation that allows everyone to evaluate and identify where they are in the process and their personal next step.

Develop Tracking Software — Make sure that critical data is being captured and evaluated so that progress can be celebrated and problems identified.

Identify Stage of Life Needs — Determine how many different stages are involved and what each stage needs for maturity. This should include identifying issues related to Christians and the unchurched as well.

Determine Best Practices Curriculum — Evaluate from all resources available what is the best product for each of the stage of life needs. This must involve the capability provided by technology both from the standpoint of best materials available and accessible on demand.

Provide Variety Channels — Establish different groups and creative delivery systems that can give people what they need when they need it with balance between relational and technology driven environments. This should also include both onsite and offsite opportunities throughout the week to maximize involvement.

Create Culture of Discipleship — Use storytelling to identify success at every stage of life and communicate through various mediums what God is doing. Changed lives should be the primary way of evaluating success and promoting all events to maximize involvement from church members and unchurched in the community.

Without alignment, there can be no sustainable process that produces spiritual maturity. Without spiritual maturity, there can be no disciples. Without disciples, we could lose three entire generations.

MINISTRY PLATFORMS

I want to take this whole concept one step deeper. I totally agree with everything in *Simple Church* about clarity, movement, alignment, and focus.

This is a great summary of their findings: "Simply stated, we found that the healthiest churches in America tended to have a simple process for making disciples. They had clarity about the process. They moved Christians intentionally through the process. They were focused on the elements of the process. And they aligned their entire congregation to this process."[7]

So, my application of this strategy is to have the entire ministry strategy outside of the worship service and special events to flow through groups, teams, or classes.

TEAMS

The church must be committed to accomplishing its stated goals through the ministry of its members. The responsibility of the staff is to equip and release church leaders to do the ministry of the church. Teams are focused on accomplishing stated goals to fulfill the ministry that God has called those involved to do.

Every ministry team should have a church leader that works with staff leadership to accomplish the team's objectives. The size of the team and its function should be suited to its specific role within the church. The qualifications for team membership can vary based on the degree of responsibility of the team.

The important point for all the leaders of teams, classes, and groups is to use your platform to help move people toward spiritual maturity. That means they need to know where every person is spiritually and make sure there is alignment on what we are asking them to do next. For example, serving on a team is an excellent entry point for many people who are "Exploring Christ." Asking a group of millennials to help support a work project in a failing inner city school is perfect alignment. Asking them to serve as an elder, obviously, is not.

The critical point here is that the role of a team leader is far more about getting "Exploring Christ" people connected and "Growing in Christ" people maturing than actually getting the work done. This is a tectonic shift in how we traditionally do church. Most staff and church leaders are put in a position where they are looking for faithful people to show up and do the job—period.

When there is a lack of high-quality leadership training and no intentionality in matching people with the right situation, then there will be massive retention issues. We waste so much time, energy, and effort because we did not do the work on the front end to find the person best fit for the position. The front-end work must include spiritual gifts and ministry profile assessments that provide information on the applicant's experience and interests. You must have a way to find the leaders God has sent you.

I have been leading new member ministry for over thirty years, so I know that the process must identify three types of people.

> **High Risk** — For a multitude of reasons, people in this category are struggling with personal problems or have been hurt or wounded recently through another church experience. The next steps for them may only be worship attendance and possibly a class. We must do whatever it takes to minister to them, and, in my experience, finding the right couple to shepherd them or involvement in a small group is a great start.

> **Low Risk** — The majority of people who will join your church fall into this category. After the new member class, it is easy to find the next best step for them. Set a reminder for a thirty-day follow up for anyone in this group.

> **High Potential** — These are high capacity leaders who will fit into one of the last two categories of spiritual maturity. If you don't get to know them soon and match them with the right service opportunity, they will leave because they don't think they are needed. Realize that God has sent these individuals to you because you need them. If you do not steward them well and just leave them sitting on the sidelines, he will send them somewhere else.

CLASSES

The primary purpose of these classes is to help people take the next step in their Christian journey. Regardless of how long someone has been a Christian, there is always a need for ongoing training.

These classes are primarily driven by the subject matter of the content that allows each person to choose which class they need. Equipping classes are usually scheduled on a semester basis and are never intended to meet the primary ministry needs of a group.

Some transformational churches have gone beyond classes and created leadership institutes. These are more highly developed courses that meet for most of the year. It is an attempt to meet the massive need for spiritual growth and leadership development.

The Village Church is one great example. The Village Church Institute (TVCI) exists to answer the question, "How can the local church effectively form disciples through transformational learning environments?" TVCI seeks to do that through a variety of environments, from one-time forums to a year-long intensive discipleship program, all centered on Christian story, Christian beliefs, and Christian formation.[8]

Training is also where the church needs to leverage technology and not require people to sit in a seat on campus for a class. People today are getting advanced degrees through online courses. We must learn to use the same technology effectively.

GROUPS

There have probably been more books written on this subject for the church than any other. The variety of approaches is wide, and I recommend that you learn from all successful models.

One of the major contextual issues for groups today is the location. The days of having large buildings where all adult groups can meet on Sunday morning are coming to an end. For some, this is clearly a financial stewardship issue. For others, it is driven by their philosophy of ministry.

The meeting environment will immediately impact the effectiveness of meeting your ministry goals. Offsite groups, whether they meet in homes, restaurants, or office buildings, will not have the same level of attendance that the onsite groups did back in the 90s. One factor is the lack of children's programming available. This, in and of itself, should not be a major limiting issue. Adults secure home childcare for everything from going out for date nights to attending ballgames out of town.

Meeting in a home immediately puts everyone in more of a community conversation mode than a classroom. This can be a very good thing if your main goal for this type of small group is building community and personal relationships. If you have people in the group who are looking for more Bible study, they may become frustrated and drop out. However, the worst thing you can do is to try to be all things to all people and end up doing nothing well.

My best advice to church leaders on this topic is to reject a one-size-fits-all approach with teams, classes, and groups. I have seen some team leaders who are great at community. I have also seen some small group leaders who are gifted teachers.

I would have some overarching guidelines for all three platforms, but I would not slap any leader on the hand for contextualizing what is best for the people under his or her leadership.

Some groups will be based on stage of life, while others will be multi-generational. Some will primarily focus on community and others on teaching or service. Some will meet once a month while others will meet weekly. Some will be large and others small.

This requires far more intentional leadership development and vision casting than you have ever done for all three platforms. The norm for church leaders is to set the priorities and require everyone to color inside the lines. I am recommending that you find great leaders and empower them to be successful. They all must understand with clarity and alignment that our shared goal is to move people toward spiritual maturity. Our effectiveness will be measured and evaluated when we see where every person in the group is in their spiritual journey compared to the same time the previous year. The information in your database combined with the stories of life change will tell you all you need to know.

MISSIONAL NETWORKS

Most churches live within a denominational affiliation that also includes its institutions and agencies. All of these groups will have different approaches on how they fund and support both the denomination and its missions in North America and throughout the world.

On one hand, you can have churches receiving appeals directly and making decisions about who receives support. The other approach is for churches to give into a combined shared fund that then makes the allocation of resources for approved institutional endeavors. I simply don't have the competency to discuss in any serious way the benefits and disadvantages of both approaches. What I see happening today is some combination of both.

Most churches have some form of cooperation within their denomination and its missional networks. Many churches are beginning to also do direct mission work that can include the appointment and support of its own missionaries. This, in my opinion, is the best approach to guarantee that your church stays in the harvest. Church leaders will need to determine the best ratio for shared and direct ministry.

There are also many new missional networks that could potentially provide help beyond your current denomination. There is nothing wrong with primarily supporting the work within your denomination while aligning with other networks. What you must accept is that you can no longer wait for all the institutional failures to be fixed before you start training every member to be a missionary. Nor can you use them as an excuse for not doing what you can and should be doing.

The Great Commandment and the Great Commission have been black ink on white paper for over 2,000 years. You cannot value the success of your denomination over the success of your local church. You must begin immediately to build your own church missional network regardless of the size of your church. It will show your community that your church is actively working to be the hands and feet of Jesus when your members are out of the building and into the harvest field.

Remember, in the past, mission work was solely for the professionals, and it was primarily done in far-away places. Today, it is for every member, and it starts right next door in our own neighborhood, in the schools we attend, and the places where we work, and it extends to anyone on the planet that needs the hope of the gospel.

If worship helps define our passion for God, then it is mission work that drives our compassion for other people.

If worship helps define our passion for God, then it is mission work that drives our compassion for other people. This sums up one of our clearest definitions of spiritual maturity: it's not about me, but all about him and them.

The foundation of the missional network is your missions team. They will develop the vision, determine the strategy, build the network, allocate resources, tell the stories, and evaluate its effectiveness.

Since you no longer are bound by making disciples that must join your church, then you must find other like-minded churches to be in your network. This is true in your city or in any village or town anywhere in the world.

It will never be enough to simply do social crisis ministry, no matter how urgent the need, if we don't find a way to move people toward the gospel. If churches do not exist there, then plant them.

Since colonialism is also dead, we want to make sure that our helping is not, in fact, hurting. For example, in Memphis, if you are a white church trying to do ministry in an African American neighborhood, you will fail in your arrogance. Find opportunities to include underperforming schools in your network. Let their leaders help you determine how you can help them without hurting. This can include everything from providing school supplies and food packs, to teacher appreciation, student tutoring, or facility improvements. Once trust has been built and ministry strategies are in place, connect them with the right church in that area and move into a support role instead. Then, find other faith-based organizations within the community that could impact this same group of students and families. Add them to your network and commit to help each other be more effective.

The next step is to seek financial support from corporate sponsors in your city that are already giving money to help the community. Identify the foundations that are constantly looking for great causes and tell them your story. Add them both to your network.

Once you become effective in your city, it may be time to move on to another school or project. This same approach can be used anywhere in the world to build effective gospel partnerships.

Once you learn how to do this well, you will need to guard against discouragement at the realization that the needs are overwhelming and the resources are limited. That is when the words of Mother Teresa will be comforting: "If you can't feed a hundred people, feed just one."[9] Over the years, this quote has led me to go deeper and stay longer with fewer ministry partners.

Now with all of the business as missions development and the use of micro loans in the third world, entire villages can be transformed for years to come. This is the ultimate holistic approach to leveraging our good works for the gospel. To help you, I will share what the latest missions team I served on developed to address all of these issues. It is aligned with everything I have shared in this chapter and will begin to merge all aspects of both the Church Gathered and Church Scattered.

MISSIONS INTEGRATION STRATEGY

Vision Casting — Develop a comprehensive strategy that makes living on mission fulltime the ultimate expression of our calling as individual disciples.

Missions Programming — Establish all missions opportunities locally, nationally, and internationally.

Missions Front Door — Use all of missions programming as front door experience to move people from community into the church.

Spiritual Formation — Acknowledge that people will be drawn to Christ and become more committed to him as they are involved in impacting other people for eternity.

Biblical Community — There is tremendous connecting and community that takes place when a group of people do something significant together.

Create Culture — Use storytelling to make helping others a way of life for every individual Christian that results in an integrated church culture and not a program to be promoted.

Develop Platforms — Identify all areas where people can connect with unchurched people in all normal traffic patterns of everyday life especially in neighborhoods and workplaces.

Church Scattered — Create an awareness and celebrate the importance of all the ministry that takes place during the week at home and in every area of our public world.

Comprehensive Training — Provide contextual training that equips every member to do cross-cultural ministry within his or her chosen platform.

Effectiveness Criteria — How many people are we helping and how many disciples are we making?

LEVERAGING TECHNOLOGY

Today, without a great website, people in your community may never visit your church. It is your front door. The overwhelming majority of people who consider coming to your church will visit your site first. If you don't prioritize this environment as much as you do your facilities, you are making a big mistake.

If you cannot stream your services, at least have high quality video recordings on your site of all aspects of your service, as well as other areas of ministry, especially preschool, children, and student ministries. Your site should also include stories about what you are doing in your city and around the world.

Now, think in terms of your discipleship matrix. What priority information do I need to communicate with specific groups to deliver best practice content? When that decision has been made, then you must decide what technology platforms are going to be the most effective. Again, this requires a targeted approach as well. Not every member should get every email blast that you send out. In my opinion, pushing information through social media or apps should be more focused on equipping members than on marketing. Providing classes on how to use YouVersion and basic Logos type apps are as important as inductive Bible study. Again, the role of the leaders is to learn to use these powerful tools and then be able to equip others.

Stop fearing the creation of a virtual church and leverage the power of technology for the kingdom. The Holy Spirit is more than capable of letting people know when they have crossed the line in sacrificing community for convenience.

Stop selling attendance and start helping with life. That's what great churches do as their role in Christianity for the 21st century.

DISRUPTIVE TRUTHS

Prioritizing the Church Scattered will help, not diminish, the Church Gathered.

Church leadership structure and culture must radically change to tear down the clergy-laity co-dependency model.

Church membership expectations must significantly change to challenge Christians to commit to an intentional discipleship process.

Small churches can be healthy again by getting members back into the harvest and leveraging technology for development.

A comprehensive discipleship process must be in place with accountability for measurable results.

Ministry platform leaders must be highly trained to contextualize their ministry to their group while supporting overall church priorities.

Church missional networks must be built that make the greatest impact possible on meeting needs in Jesus' name.

Chapter Six: Church Scattered

I hope by now you are getting a clear picture of what Church Scattered means. It is not an attempt to create two competing churches—there is only one Church, one Lord, and one Mission. The use of the term "Church Scattered" is a way for Christians to prioritize the ministry that occurs during Monday through Saturday without minimizing the one day when we gather. It's not an either/or approach but a both/and approach. Just like we have come to use new terms like "teaching pastors" and "multi-site," leaders can use "Church Gathered" and "Church Scattered" to elevate the priority of both.

The Father has always wanted to be represented to the world through his people not a place. When most people hear the word "church" today, they automatically think about the place where we meet on Sundays. We need to intentionally and aggressively change that cultural paradigm both for Christians and unchurched people. In the future, we want the word "church" to primarily refer to Christians in the workplace and community.

In the future, we want the word "church" to primarily refer to Christians in the workplace and community.

For my entire lifetime, we have placed more priority on *attending* church than *being* the church. That naturally means that staff leaders are compelled to place a higher priority on what happens when we come together than when we are apart, too.

My experience is that we have placed up to 80 percent of our resources on supporting what we know as the Church Gathered and only 20 percent directly for the Church Scattered. I am advocating that we move at least 70 percent of our resources into the ministries that directly support the Church Scattered.

This would mean that resources on personal Bible study, biblical worldview, work-faith integration, marriage, parenting, and storytelling all in a cross-cultural context would move up the priority list.

An intentional priority on individual responsibility and discipleship next steps would be established and monitored for progress that occurs in the Church Scattered. The role of staff leaders changes from people doing ministry to leaders equipping other leaders to support the entire mission of the church.

Placing a higher priority on the Church Scattered will require a transformational shift in the roles of leaders in the church and Christians in the marketplace. In *Transformational Church,* Ed Stetzer and Thom Rainer write, "When the church assumes the role of missionary, a radical shift in the view of leadership must take place. The old model was to hoard and retain control. Transformational leaders seek to empower and multiply."[1]

According to Stetzer and Rainer, there are four shifts that must take place:

1. The first mindset shift is from *one* to *many* leaders. This shared leadership model is critical for alignment and empowerment.

2. The second shift is from *me* to *we*. Leaders are called to help develop other leaders who know and exercise their spiritual gifts in every area of life.

3. The third mindset shift is from *personal power* to *people empowerment*. The leaders must be secure in their own calling before they will give others permission to be successful in theirs.

4. The fourth is from *church* to *the kingdom*. The success of the kingdom must become a higher priority than what happens in a single local church.

They drive all of this home with the following: "With the advent of church buildings, the temptation was to become building-focused, inward, self-absorbed congregations. People became spectators. Scattering throughout the community as the church was replaced with the sacred, passive gathering in one place. The building and activities of the church at times became more important than God's greater kingdom."[2]

When church leaders become willing to pass the baton to Christians, we must be prepared to take it and make all parts of our lives sacred. Because the Holy Spirit lives within you, he can make any place sacred—from the car rides to school to the multiple meetings we attend every day.

In *Breaking the Missional Code* Stetzer and Rainer do an incredible job in dealing with both of these mindset shifts that need to occur:

- *From programs to processes*
- *From demographics to discernment*
- *From models to missions*
- *From attractional to incarnational*
- *From uniformity to diversity*
- *From professional to passionate*
- *From seating to sending*
- *From decisions to disciples*
- *From monuments to movements*[3]

Dan Kimball calls it a shift from "I am going to church" to "I am the church." In *The Emerging Church*, he writes, "Church is seen as a body of people sent on a mission who gather in community for worship, encouragement, and teaching from the Word that supplements what they are feeding themselves throughout the week."[4] The focus of the last chapter was to help church leaders in several critical areas that need transformational change. I want to spend the rest of this chapter on the individual changes Christians must make to become fully devoted followers of Christ and servant leaders of others in the Church Scattered. I'm going to cover some key areas where your thinking will need to significantly shift to be effective in the Church Scattered, both in your beliefs and your behavior. This will also lay the foundation for the final three chapters of practical application.

LEADERSHIP DEVELOPMENT

One of the most significant transformations that must occur is that you, as an individual Christian, must assume the personal responsibility for your growing relationship with Christ.

This part of the church membership covenant lays this out:

> I will commit to assume a personal responsibility for my own spiritual growth and that of my family. In making this commitment, I will take the following personal actions in my own life (I John 2:12-14; 1 Peter 2:2; Deut. 6:4-9):

> I will complete a personal spiritual evaluation tool with my coach that will determine the next steps to help me move in my spiritual journey.

> I will identify a person who will be a relational accountability partner to me. This person could come from a class, group, team, or a spiritual coach provided by the church, or someone in my life who is currently serving in this role.

> I will participate throughout the year in the next steps that have been identified to help me grow spiritually and reevaluate with my accountability partner once a year to determine my progress and set new goals for the next year.

There is no more outsourcing to church leaders your responsibility as a Christian for Bible study, prayer, marriage, parenting, missions, or calling. They are now there to support you and help equip you to fulfill your biblical calling in life. Work and faith, as well as leadership and life, are all integrated so that you can know Christ and make him known.

The way this has worked best for me as a Christian leader who is a committed disciple, is to divide all of my responsibilities into three major areas: *Personal*, *Private*, and *Public*. Again, we will fully develop all three areas in the last section of the book.

First, I recommend the development of a Life Plan that will allow you to set priorities in every area and then specific measurable goals for progress. It is assumed that you are fully committed by now to merge faith and work so that all of the secular parts of your life can become sacred.

One of the most significant transformations that must occur is that you, as an individual Christian, must assume the personal responsibility for your growing relationship with Christ.

The next step is to fully merge leadership and life. Leaders identify priorities, set goals, develop strategies, cast vision, solve problems, and measure results.

The good news is that every leadership best practice ultimately comes from God, and he will help you take all that you have learned at work and use it at home. In the same way, he will also take every biblical truth you learned—humility, honesty, integrity, commitment, feedback, and servant leadership—and teach you to become a better leader at work.

I have a priority to lead myself first, and I simply call this my *Personal* leadership area. This includes making sure I have all the spiritual, emotional, and physical margin I need to meet the needs of others in my life.

The second major area is my immediate family, and I call this my *Private* leadership area. This involves all that I am biblically given to do in leading my marriage and parenting my children for the rest of my life. (Sorry, the parenting jar of marbles that you've been told slowly empties is fake news—you're a parent for life.)

The third major area is my *Public* leadership area. This includes anything involving work, friends, neighbors, extended family, and church.

It is critical to point out that there is an order of prioritization that cannot be compromised for you to be successful. If you don't put your spiritual growth as the top priority in your *Personal* life, then everything else will fail. This will require developing an intentional plan to ensure this happens.

Then, in your *Private* world you must place your spouse in the number two priority slot and your children in the third, or, regardless of what else you accomplish in life, you will have missed God's calling.

One thing to note: I did not say there is any guarantee that, just because you do your part, other people will automatically do the same. Marriages fail and children rebel regardless of how well you lead yourself or your family.

However, if you are leading well in your *Personal* and *Private* worlds then the *Public* responsibilities will become significantly easier to lead. Although the *Public* leadership area may demand the most time, it must not be the top priority.

We as individual Christians have the same resource allocation crisis as the Church Gathered. We can allocate up to 80 percent of our margin to the *Public* area, only to be left with 20 percent for the priorities and people that matter most.

It takes great personal leadership to know the difference between something that is urgent and something that is important. You have to develop the spiritual maturity as a leader to fit all the big rocks in the jar first.

To the degree that you learn to follow Christ, you will have the power to lead others. And, to the degree that you are under his authority, you can be over others.

Remember, during the final performance review at the end of your life, the conversation will only be about you and him. So, regardless of how others respond, you can still hear the most rewarding words ever spoken about your life: "Well done, my good and faithful servant."

RELATIONAL NETWORK

There are many different roles you will play as a Christian living in the Church Scattered. First, you are a committed disciple who prioritizes knowing Christ and making him known. You are also a servant leader to your family and a "Good Samaritan" to all who need your help. To accomplish everything else that you are called to do outside of this, you must also become a fulltime missionary.

We set all of this up in Chapter Two by introducing the idea that we have three generations in America who are as culturally distant from God as anyone living in India or Iran. This contextual reality demands a cross-cultural relational approach to effectively reach people for Christ.

For it to be relational, it must be intentional. You need to build relationships with lost people that will build trust over time so they can more effectively hear and respond to the gospel.

This includes people at work, living in your neighborhood, cutting your hair, your insurance agent, or anyone else you can establish a relationship with in the normal everyday patterns of life. I intentionally bought three sets of tires over an eight-year window from the same man to help move him toward Christ. I have been using the same barber for more than ten years for the very same reason. I am intentionally developing relationships with several of my neighbors every chance I get.

The key here is not to have hundreds of lost people in your network; you don't have the time to have meaningful conversations with that many people. However, the Holy Spirit may assign up to twenty or so people who you will pray for every day to come to know Christ.

I started this relational network to help keep track of all the people I am ministering to in my *Public* world. Other Christians are in this network as well, with an appropriate level of ministry defined. This network is a prayer journal on steroids.

This is merely an extension to what most of us do in the corporate world when we create and sustain a professional network. You are now using those same personal leadership skills to integrate faith into all of your relationships.

It becomes a necessity to use some software application that will allow you to pray for and minister to this group. I assign certain categories that determine how often I pray and connect based on their needs. For example, if someone on the list is a friend living in another city who lost a child to cancer, I make sure to reach out to them on that date every year.

As a trained missionary you will be able over time to use discernment and wisdom to accurately determine where every person is on this scale as presented in Chapter Two:

> *Hostile: Harmful experiences in the past and are bitter toward God and the church.*

> *Negative: Someone or something has hurt them, and they have not forgotten.*

> *Indifferent: No interest at all; their mindset is "I don't want to talk about it."*

> *Neutral: No strong feelings or thoughts either way.*

> *Open: Usually willing to listen but not commit.*

> *Interest: Seeking to process faith and hope it will work for them.*

> *Receptive: Grateful that God has sent someone to help them find Christ.*

The next critical factor is that you must make the commitment to find ways to be in their life. You may be thinking, "I just don't have the time for this." The point I'm trying to make is, for the most part, you're already doing it. The key is to be intentional when you go about your normal patterns of everyday life.

There was a time when I would ask my small group things like, "Does anyone know a good Christian auto mechanic?" Now, I intentionally seek out a lost person so that I can create a relational connection. When you are "all in" as a committed disciple, the need for eternal salvation trumps financial stewardship and customer service. We must seek out the lost where they work and live, because they're not coming to our churches.

I fully admit the increased level of ministry for which I am advocating will require an extra commitment of time. And, for most of us, so will prioritizing personal Bible study, our marriage, and parenting.

The next major truth any missionary understands is that all of us, including our lost friends, are changed by major life events:

Death of a loved one
Divorce or separation
College graduation

Marriage
Pregnancy
Birth of a child
Parenting
Loss of job
Moving to another city
Major health problems
Empty nest
Retirement

The truth is, we are all affected to some degree by these major life changes. Even for Christians, some of these experiences can either lead to brokenness or bitterness.

In building our relational network, we should take extra care with those experiencing major life changes. In my own life, I am ashamed to admit I have often failed in this ministry area. On the third conversation with a lost neighbor, I learned where he worked and the names of his wife and children, only to forget. I have also gained enough trust with a lost co-worker to have them come to me and tell me their wife was having surgery, only to see him at a meeting after the fact and realize I forgot to pray for or check on her. What a massive withdrawal of their trust and failure in my personal responsibility.

I'm encouraging you to build a strong relational network so that this won't happen to you as you minister in the Church Scattered. Now that I'm intentional, I've also experienced the blessing of seeing tears roll down someone's face when I unexpectedly showed up to visit them in the hospital.

The Holy Spirit wants to use us in these powerful change points in someone's life to move them in a positive direction toward Christ. My prayer with every interaction is to make sure I am making spiritual deposits with acts of kindness and encouraging words. These become some of the most sacred moments in our life when we are given the opportunity to represent the hands and feet of Christ.

As a Spirit-empowered missionary, you will have the wisdom and confidence to supernaturally align how receptive they are, the change point, the setting, and the appropriate ministry. My goal is to leave everyone that I encounter a little better than I found them. I want people to see Christ in me through my attitude and actions.

I will share just one personal story that worked by the grace of God. We had been cultivating a relationship with a neighbor couple for at least two years. My wife and I had shared our stories about how we came to know Christ. They knew we were Christians but not completely sure what that meant. One afternoon, they came over for a visit and brought us a very nice bottle of wine as a gift. The problem was,

These become some of the most sacred moments in our life when we are given the opportunity to represent the hands and feet of Christ.

we don't drink alcohol. Before you tune me out, the alcohol debate is not the point of this story. This is about how to maintain your own biblical convictions without losing relational trust with those you're trying to reach. If you become serious about representing Christ in the midst of the Church Scattered, you will be faced with these types of decisions.

Now, I could have poured it out and risked the question of "how did you enjoy the wine?" Or, just as bad, engaged in a self-righteous judgmental debate on drinking alcohol.

Instead, my wife and I prayed about what to do and settled on maintaining our trust with the couple by telling the truth. Later that day, I sincerely thanked them for the wonderfully kind gesture and told them I would not dare waste such a great gift. I wanted to return it because, even though I did not personally drink wine, I still valued their relationship most of all.

The Holy Spirit did what only he can do.

Several months later, their trust and our commitment were put to the test. We were invited to a party in their home and were told on the front end there would be alcohol served. We happily accepted the invitation to the party and visited well into the evening to make sure we did not waste their trust in our relationship.

After many more conversations, there was no doubt they had moved from "neutral" into the "open" and "interested" stage of receptivity. Several months later, we moved to Atlanta, and I was grateful to the Father for using us in such a small way to plant and water the gospel seed in their lives.

The ministry in the Church Scattered is messy and it can take years for someone to move from "negative" to "interested" in hearing your story. The most significant investment you will make in their lives will be the hours you spend praying for them to come to Christ.

I personally believe of all the titles our Savior had, the one he loved the most was "friend of sinners." He was right at home in a party full of lost people.

So, when I take Christ with me to meet and greet corporate events, there is a divine presence that I do not experience anywhere else. The yoke is on, the burden is light, and my soul is at rest.

CHURCH PLANTING

This is going to be another controversial area where I am integrating a well-defined practice with a totally transformational application. Traditional church planting of the Church Gathered model is a hot topic anyway with many varied opinions on strategy and best practices.

The churches that I want to be planted are ministries of the Church Scattered. In these churches, we will not be having corporate worship with congregational singing, expository preaching, communion, or baptism. These church plants involve Christians working together to accomplish the mission of Christ at work and in their neighborhoods. These are not formally recognized as churches but, informally, are performing the ministry of the Church Gathered.

FAMILY MINISTRY

For example, I see my personal family ministry as a church plant. When we gather for a shared meal, the kitchen becomes a sacred place. Fellowship occurs in a deeply faith-based community. Biblical truths are shared in the context of all of our daily lives. The personal conversations are centered on how God is working in our lives and how we can pray for each other.

This is the context where the fruit of my personal faith walk is expressed to the fullest. I am charged with loving my wife unconditionally and bringing my children up in the discipline and instruction of the Lord. The family is the primary place where biblical discipleship happens. There is a time for instruction in truth, but the most powerful moments are when grace is given and not deserved. I am to be a human expression of the divine reality in their lives.

I am not diminishing the value of the Church Gathered in my family by elevating my responsibility in this expression of the Church Scattered. This level of prioritization demands that I step up spiritually and become a fully devoted follower of Christ.

Any movement to create family churches that are exclusively led by fathers who see themselves as the pastor of their family is also unbiblical. But, in our society, many men do not see themselves as the spiritual leaders at all because of character and competency issues and are ashamed to admit it. The guilt can be overwhelming, and, many times, men will respond in anger or withdraw. They will outsource the spiritual leadership to their wives, creating a dysfunctional culture that will not work. Wives try to fill that spiritual leadership void, and, by doing that, are placing themselves in the slot where their husbands should be. This never ends well.

For any family church plant of the Church Scattered to work, everyone needs to get back in their lane. Stop trying to "fix" your spouse and trust God to work through you and in them:

> Wives, submit to your husbands, as is fitting in the Lord. Husbands, love your wives, and do not be harsh with them. Children, obey your parents in everything, for this pleases the Lord. Fathers, do not provoke your children, lest they become discouraged. (Colossians 3:18-2)

These church plants involve Christians working together to accomplish the mission of Christ at work and in their neighborhoods.

This will be your greatest challenge and highest calling. There is nothing that the corporate world or culture can offer you that can begin to compare in importance.

If for any reason you are still thinking that the qualifications for being a pastor, deacon, or missionary are greater than the roles of husband, father, wife, and mother, you are wrong. This will be your greatest challenge and highest calling. There is nothing that the corporate world or culture can offer you that can begin to compare in importance. So, commit to leading well.

NEIGHBORHOOD MINISTRY

The second place I want to see more churches planted is in our neighborhoods. This is your local circle and the cultural receptivity for lost people is higher here than anywhere else. Here again, you cannot know all of your neighbors in a deeply relational way. So, pray for those that God wants you to get to know better.

This network will include other Christians who will at times need your ministry. Young couples need older Christians in their lives and can use the encouragement and advice.

In my own relational network, there are two widows that have a special place in my heart. Some have good families that help take care of them and some do not.

There is no tension here in trying to replace the Church Gathered in their life. This is not a setup to be able to invest and then invite them to your church. This is simply the body of Christ ministering to each other in a Church Scattered context. The real challenge is to not let the ministry to fellow Christians take the place of time spent with those who do not know Christ. Typically, at least 70 percent of my network includes people who do not know Christ.

Missionaries learn how to meet people in the normal everyday traffic patterns of life. In my experience, the summertime will give you more opportunities than any other time of the year outside of major holidays. My greatest success over the years has been to connect with people while I am out exercising. This is one of the reasons I don't like gym memberships—I would miss divine appointments with neighbors.

When I speak to people in my neighborhood, I get everything from "Have a blessed day" to no response at all. "Have a blessed day" in Memphis is code for "I am a Christian." I continue to be polite to those individuals, but rarely do they make it to my network database. My goal, after learning their name, is to find out a little of their story. In our culture that is so impersonal at times, it can be a powerful thing to see someone and call them by name.

I know many of you think this sounds too basic to even discuss. But I want to remind you of the process the Holy Spirit uses to bring someone to faith. Our role is to plow the fields. This is my ongoing intentional ministry of trying to connect in a personal way with another person. I will also remind you that many of these people are hostile or negative toward faith. They may be bitter toward God and trust no one. Once you make the connection and learn their name, you can begin to sow seeds of truth and grace. Then, you will begin to water them with your daily prayers and seek opportunities to move them closer to Christ.

Recently, I began to cross paths every morning with a young African American man. (I tell you that only to make the point that I am, well, an old white guy who he probably wouldn't hang out with!) For at least the first three times I said, "Good morning," he never lifted his head. This is where prayer becomes critical to discern whether you need to back off or lean in. I leaned in and added, "I hope you have a great day." After two months of slow progress, one morning I turned the corner and he was nowhere in sight. To my absolute delight, he was walking behind me and yelled out "Good morning" to me instead. I decided to take one more step and stopped to talk with him. I now know his name, where he works, and his strong handshake. After he walked on, all of that information went immediately into my phone database so that I could pray for him.

Over the years, some of these relationships have progressed to the point that I've been asked to get the mail, let out the dogs, and move all manner of furniture. When you're invited into someone's home or they've been in yours, you are making massive deposits.

I look for opportunities to cut my neighbor's grass when I know they are on vacation. A critical learned truth that works for anyone in your network including family—do not tell them it was you who did it. This allows the Holy Spirit to use the ministry for the maximum impact. Grace means that they probably don't deserve the act of kindness, and you certainly don't deserve the credit.

Once I have reached the level of connection where trust has been built, I take the next step. This could happen on the first meeting or it could take over a year. I ask if I can pray about an issue in their life. Now, I have just brought faith into the relationship, and it will not be long before I share the story of how I came to know Christ and what he means to me.

After I share my gospel story, I don't ask if they are a Christian or where they go to church. Just like in my corporate experience in coaching, I simply ask them what role faith plays in their life.

If you want to go deeper in this ministry, I would suggest joining your neighborhood homeowners association. Get to know the leaders and offer, if appropriate, to be the chaplain for the community. This would be an incredible ministry opportunity. The even deeper end of the pool is to offer to lead a Bible study on the life of Jesus Christ in a home. Invite everyone and get ready for one of the most challenging and rewarding experiences of your life.

Saying "Good morning," cutting the grass, and praying for someone is not the gospel. It is a critical part of plowing, sowing, and watering the soil so the gospel can be heard.

I have only personally seen a few people move all the way to a saving faith in Christ through neighborhood ministry. I am absolutely confident though that I have seen hundreds move closer to Christ.

MARKETPLACE MINISTRY

The cultural context is somewhat challenging, but the scale of the ministry platform is massive. The fields are white unto harvest, but we desperately need more laborers.

When you fully integrate faith and work, then you can begin to plant churches in your workplace and with the people under your influence.

I want to remind you of something I said in the Introduction: Chick-fil-A has had more moral influence on this pagan post-Christian culture in America than any church or denomination. I view every CFA restaurant as having the potential to be a plant of the Church Scattered. Their recent high-profile foundation problems do not diminish their potential for influence. In fact, it increases it. CFA leaders must realize they are selling far more than chicken.

I know many godly men and women who lead these ministry outposts. They would never say of themselves what I'm about to say. However, when you hear their passion and see their good works, they are intentionally moving people toward Christ.

Take a look at the core values and mission of just a few:

Tyson Foods

"Be honorable and operate with integrity; Be faith-friendly and inclusive; Serve as stewards of the resources entrusted to us; Provide a safe work environment."

Their vision statement is stronger than many churches: *"From the beginning, our company has been built on faith, family, and hard work. That tradition, our Core Values, and 'doing what's right' are deeply embedded in our culture. -John Tyson, Chairman*[5]

Hobby Lobby

"Honoring the Lord in all we do by operating the company in a manner consistent with Biblical principles. Offering our customers exceptional selection and value. Serving our employees and their families by establishing a work environment and company policies that build character, strengthen individuals, and nurture families. Providing a return on the family's investment, sharing the Lord's blessings with our employees,

and investing in our community."[6]

Barnhart Crane, Memphis, TN

"The purpose of Barnhart Crane and Rigging Co. is to glorify God by providing an opportunity for His people to use their skills and gifts in His service through constructive work, personal witness and ministry funding.

One of Barnhart's stated core values is important for all of these plants of the Church Scattered—profit with a purpose. *"We will attempt to make profit and will invest the profit to expand the company and to meet the needs of others (physically, mentally, spiritually)."[7]*

These plants of the Church Scattered have a biblical stewardship of making a profit to then, in turn, make a difference. They have more of a holistic approach toward caring for employees and their families, meeting the needs of the poor, and benefitting their city than most churches I know.

As I said, the tip of the spear now in the 10/40 window is not a missions agency but businesses as missions where Christian executives are starting companies so they can effectively plant new churches. A personal friend of mine in Memphis has done just that. The name of the company is Highland Harvesters and this is their mission:

Recognizing the biblical model of Paul's tentmaking enterprise and the historical example of other tentmaker missionaries since the time of the Reformation, Highland Harvesters desires to build businesses through which business minded missionaries can share the Gospel with their employees and the community. In so doing, we want to show others that tentmaking is not simply a means to be in the mission context, but the ministry itself. Highland Harvesters is an agribusiness that accomplishes the following:

Transitions an American missionary, Jonathan Bridges, from needing to raise annual financial support to supporting himself and his ministry.

Provides a platform for Jonathan Bridges and other Ethiopian Christian businessmen to share the Gospel and disciple others.

Models for other missionaries how to be a tentmaker.

Allows other Christians to invest in Kingdom businesses.

Creates a highly visible business presence in Ethiopia.

Generates significant profit to expand the business and ministry.[8]

Please notice that these are not businesses that are doing ministry. The full integration of faith and work means that the business platform is the ministry.

There is no doubt that the gospel effectiveness of these marketplace plants is directly impacted by the spiritual maturity of their Christian leaders. However, the same thing can be said about every church, family, and neighborhood ministry as well.

I like to call these marketplace Christian leaders "corporate shepherds." They may be the CEO of a large company like Tyson Foods or Hobby Lobby, or they may be a manager in a small company with ten people under their direct influence. The spiritual qualifications are exactly the same—to be a fully devoted follower of Christ and a servant leader of others. Their passion is to know Christ and then to make him known.

Also, if you are one of these corporate shepherds, God has not called you to be their pastor and any attempt to fill that role is destined to fail. You are never to fill the role of the Church Gathered regardless of your capability or desire to do so.

All of the missionary training surrounding receptivity axis, change points, and the development of intentional relationships is even more critical in this context. There is a tremendous difference between connecting with a neighbor and leading an employee. You will need to add all of these people into your relational network. My network includes clients, co-workers, neighbors, and friends.

One of the significant differences between neighborhood and marketplace ministries is that, at work, you will need to allow more time for Christians. The opportunities for discipleship many times can be greater than evangelism. That is why you will hear of so many volunteer Bible studies being offered in the workplace. A lot of lunch and learn opportunities are offering character development training that is almost identical to spiritual maturity.

I have seen company's partner with Compassion International and commit to match every dollar given by employees to help with orphans all over the world. They then send a team of employees to that year's project who come back with stories that are shared in an employee meeting.

The ministry of the Church Scattered within a workplace culture is a powerful tool in reaching these three lost generations. Both Christians and the unchurched will be "all in" for making a profit so they can make an even greater difference.

SPIRITUAL WARFARE

This is certainly not a happy subject but a necessary one for any Christian who is committed to serving in the Church Scattered. Part of the reason is due to the massive cultural disruption discussed earlier in the book.

Being a committed Christian was once considered to be a socially good thing and would give people a favorable impression of an individual. Today, if you live out your faith, you can be seen as intolerant at best and a terrorist at worst.

Jesus warned us about all of this:

> If you were of the world, the world would love you as its own; but because you are not of the world, but I chose you out of the world, therefore the world hates you. Remember the word that I said to you: 'A servant is not greater than his master.' If they persecuted me, they will also persecute you. (John 15:19-20)

For years, I had this all so wrong and was not willing to admit what was really happening and why. Like many Christians during hard times, I would say that the devil was attacking me. The reality was that I was not doing anything supernatural or impactful that would require even one demon to be assigned to attack me. I was just suffering the consequences of my own disobedience.

> For this is a gracious thing, when, mindful of God, one endures sorrows while suffering unjustly. For what credit is it if, when you sin and are beaten for it, you endure? But if when you do good and suffer for it you endure, this is a gracious thing in the sight of God. For to this you have been called, because Christ also suffered for you, leaving you an example, so that you might follow in his steps. (1 Peter 2:19-21)

I had clearly been suffering for sin's sake and my level of spiritual maturity knew nothing of suffering for righteousness sake. It's at this very point where the Holy Spirit will use us the most. When your co-workers see you get solely blamed for a major project failure when it was actually not your fault, and you say nothing, that is powerful. When you do the right thing and suffer for it, and the only one who knows the truth is the Father, that is even better.

Back then, I would never think about daily putting on the armor of God because I wasn't doing anything that would require it. Then, when I would still refuse to repent of my sin, things would get worse. Surely the devil himself must be involved this time, I thought. No, the author of all my storms at this point was not the devil but the Creator.

He loves us too much to leave us in our sin, and he will do whatever it takes to change us:

> Consider him who endured from sinners such hostility against himself, so that you may not grow weary or fainthearted. In your struggle against sin you have not yet resisted to

"

The ministry of the Church Scattered within a workplace culture is a powerful tool in reaching these three lost generations. Both Christians and the unchurched will be "all in" for making a profit so that they can make an even greater difference.

> *When you try to rescue children out of human trafficking and help redeem anyone out of the domain of darkness, you are walking in enemy-occupied territory.*

the point of shedding your blood. And have you forgotten the exhortation that addresses you as sons?

"My son, do not regard lightly the discipline of the Lord, nor be weary when reproved by him. For the Lord disciplines the one he loves, and chastises every son whom he receives."

It is for discipline that you have to endure. God is treating you as sons. For what son is there whom his father does not discipline? If you are left without discipline, in which all have participated, then you are illegitimate children and not sons. Besides this, we have had earthly fathers who disciplined us and we respected them. Shall we not much more be subject to the Father of spirits and live? For they disciplined us for a short time as it seemed best to them, but he disciplines us for our good, that we may share his holiness. For the moment all discipline seems painful rather than pleasant, but later it yields the peaceful fruit of righteousness to those who have been trained by it. (Hebrews 12:3-11)

Once you realize that the struggle to go to church on Sunday is probably not spiritual warfare, then you can own your disobedience and move beyond conviction and chastisement. What will come next will be all-out war—a subject that must be taken very seriously.

Put on the whole armor of God, that you may be able to stand against the schemes of the devil. For we do not wrestle against flesh and blood, but against the rulers, against the authorities, against the cosmic powers over this present darkness, against the spiritual forces of evil in the heavenly places. (Ephesians 6:11-12)

If the phrase "against the cosmic powers over this present darkness and the spiritual forces of evil in the heavenly places" does not scare you, then you don't understand. When you try to rescue children out of human trafficking and help redeem anyone out of the domain of darkness, you are walking in enemy-occupied territory.

However, God has not given us a spirit of fear and we know that the one who lives in us is greater than he that is in the world. He has sent us on the mission of redemption and restoration with all of his power and authority to be more than conquerors through him that loves us.

Christian missionaries have been dealing with this level of spiritual warfare for centuries. Now, maybe, because the time is short, this open evil hostility is being directed toward Christians in North America. Welcome to Christianity for the 21st century.

DISRUPTIVE TRUTHS

The Church Gathered and the Church Scattered are one church with the same mission.

The number one priority of every Christian must be a growing relationship with Christ through Bible study and prayer.

The development of a relational network will allow you to intentionally meet the needs of others during the most difficult times in their life.

Making appropriate grace-based deposits into the lives of lost people will help in moving them closer to Christ.

Becoming a church planter will allow you to develop strategies that will help people in your family, neighborhood, and workplace to experience Christ living through you.

The days of persecution and suffering for righteousness sake are here and we must be prepared for nothing less than warfare.

Chapter Seven: Personal Leadership

In this final section of the book, we are going to maximize the application of truth into our daily lives. The practical tools I will offer will primarily be based on what has worked for me over the years. Let's begin with what I believe is the most important subject of all—personal leadership.

You may not consider yourself to be in a leadership position at work, but we are all leaders of ourselves. As Christians, we are also called to lead well in our marriages and with our children. The priority, now that you have merged work and faith, is to merge leadership and life. The clearest expression of who God has purposed you to be is in the role of a Christian leader.

The one thing about leadership that has never changed is that you must learn to lead yourself first before you can effectively lead other people. A reminder of my favorite leadership quote by Thomas Watson: "Nothing so conclusively proves a man's ability to lead others as what he does from day to day to lead himself."[1]

I want to challenge you to be committed to excellence in every area of your life both personally and professionally to fulfill the mission of representing God to the world. The core values that we hold will directly determine our definition of success in all of life. We can either live out the script that others have written for us, or we will have the courage to write our own. My passion is to motivate you to be willing to pay the price to define what you want your legacy to be for the people and priorities that you care about the most. Quite frankly, when it is all said and done, that is all that really matters.

One of my favorite things to do is hike. To me, a hiker is somewhere between a camper and an adventure racer. One of the great advantages of living in the Atlanta area for ten years was the close proximity to the Appalachian Trail in the north Georgia mountains.

My favorite hiking story comes from the owner of a beautiful resthouse along a hiking trail in the Swiss Alps. On this particular trail, if you start early in the morning, you can reach the summit and be back to your car before dark. The owner of the resthouse has noticed an interesting pattern over the years. When the hikers arrive, everyone is excited and determined to reach the summit. Once they've eaten lunch, rested, and warmed themselves by the fire, someone in the group inevitably says what everyone else is thinking: "You guys go ahead without me, and I will join you on the way back down the trail." Then, everyone in the group is faced with the decision to stay or go. For those who stay, the first few hours are enjoyable. They sit by the fire and share mountain-climbing stories and reminisce about past hiking experiences.

My passion is to motivate you to be willing to pay the price to define what you want your legacy to be for the people and priorities that you care about the most.

By early afternoon, the mood dramatically changes, and everyone gets quiet. One by one, they make their way over to the window in the back of the lodge and stare at the summit. It's in this regret-filled moment they realize they have settled for second best.

I wonder how many times we've felt that same way over missed opportunities.

I don't want to settle for average in any area of my life. I know that sinless perfection is not attainable, but we should strive every day to become more and more like the image of Christ.

We have been told to redeem the time because the days are evil. We don't want to look back with regrets because we valued things over people and the pleasures of this life over the rewards of eternity.

William Lewis has well said, "The tragedy of life is not that it ends so soon, but that we wait so long to begin it."[2]

I want this book to be a resthouse moment for you. When you finish it, I want your appreciation for the unsearchable riches of Christ to bring you to a "but one thing I do" moment:

> *Not that I have already obtained this or am already perfect,*
> *but I press on to make it my own, because Christ Jesus has*
> *made me his own. Brothers, I do not consider that I have made it my own.*
> *But one thing I do: forgetting what lies behind and straining forward*
> *to what lies ahead, I press on toward the goal for the prize of the*
> *upward call of God in Christ Jesus. (Philippians 3:12-14)*

Phillip Brooks has said, "Sad is that day for any person when he or she becomes absolutely satisfied with the life they are living, the thoughts they are thinking, and the deeds they are doing; until there ceases to be forever beating at the door of their soul a desire to do something large which they seek and know they were meant and intended to do."[3]

My hometown for all practical purposes is Tuscumbia, Alabama. Tuscumbia's one and only claim to fame is that it is the birthplace of Helen Keller. Keller, as you know, was deaf and blind. Despite these incredible obstacles, she found a way to fulfill her calling and reach her potential. She was once asked, "Can you think of anything worse than being born blind?" Her response was a powerful one: "Yes, to have sight and lack vision."[4]

My prayer is that you are beginning to develop a clear vision for what the Father has called you to do with your life and that you are fully committed to that mission.

This is where, as a Christian leader, a clear set of biblical priorities, strategies, goals, and evaluation come as our appropriate next step.

I want to use both leadership and biblical truth to set up this next step. We have already acknowledged how disrupted our lives are and the stress that it causes. Church Scattered is not about adding more activity to an already overpacked schedule. It is about total biblical alignment of your entire life. That alignment will give you renewed purpose and create more margin in every area.

GRACE ACCOUNT

A leadership concept I use in executive coaching is the priority of margin. Margin is the difference between the demands that are coming into your life and your capacity to meet them. These factors can change multiple times a day.

We need margin spiritually, emotionally, and physically every day to accomplish what is really important. When we have no margin in an area, we either have to reduce demands, increase capacity, or both.

To reduce demand, we have to be able to say "no" to something for a bigger "yes." If you have not defined the bigger priorities, then it is impossible to know what to say "no" to. This results in full calendars and very empty lives.

A critical truth in living the Christian life is that it was designed by the Father to be lived out one day at a time. We desperately want to be able to see and know beyond just the present day, but that would not require faith, and faith is a big deal to God.

He will give you the spiritual version of margin called "grace" to have the power to accomplish what he wants for that day. He already knows what will happen and he promises to provide exactly the right amount. It's kind of a New Testament manna thing (with all apologies to Andy Stanley).

Our responsibility in this relationship is to make sure we don't waste today's grace on something that was not on the Father's "yes" list for today. When we do waste the grace, we run out of what we needed for today and we crash.

(I acknowledged that I am from Alabama, so this has to be simple for me to grasp.)

For this to work, there are three critical truths that you must apply every day:

Forgiveness for the past: If you have not completely forgiven someone of something that was done in the past, you can waste today's grace by still thinking about your pain. The often-missed first step is to ask for your own forgiveness from the Father regardless of how someone else hurt you. Their actions can never be an excuse for your anger and bitterness. The biblical reality is that you cannot compare what someone has done to you to what Christ has done for you.

Faith for the future: The other major enemy of today's grace is worrying about the future. When we worry, we are placing more faith in our own logic and reason than God's providence and provision. A simple test for me is that if I am thinking about something far more than I am praying about it, then I am still the one trying to fix it. We can't "give it" to the Father in one prayer and then almost immediately take it back.

Grace for today: The Father never calls you to do anything that he will not empower you to accomplish. We are doing way too many things that he has not called us to do, and we are daily demeaning his character in front of the whole world by not trusting him. Again, how can we possibly say that God can be trusted for eternity but not for today? The only conclusion would be that he is either unable or unwilling to help today. Both are lies of the enemy and appeal to our pride that tells us we can handle this without his grace.

LIFE PLAN

The next step for every Christian is the development of your Life Plan. It is an absolute necessity to accomplish all that the Father wants you to do in every area of your life. This will mean defining your priorities and setting specific measurable goals. One of the most important truths that must be understood is the difference between goals and desires.

A goal should be something where you primarily can control the outcome. Stephen Covey calls this your "circle of influence." I can set a goal to spend thirty minutes every morning in Bible study and prayer.[5]

A desire, on the other hand, is something I prayerfully want to happen for the right reasons, but, in the end, I cannot control the outcome. Covey calls this your "circle of concern." For example, I want my children to love God, but I cannot make them trust him with their life.

This will also drive the spiritual discipline of making sure we are always setting realistic expectations. The setting of unrealistic expectations will lead to more relational conflict than anything else in every area of your life. You and the Father are in a partnership. He wants you to prioritize your relationship with him and to never try to fill his role in someone else's life.

Covey will challenge you to develop your own personal version of your biblical worldview. How do you know something is important and how will you accomplish it consistently in your life?

> *To reduce demand, we have to be able to say "no" to something for a bigger "yes." If you have not defined the bigger priorities, then it is impossible to know what to say "no" to. This results in full calendars and very empty lives.*

These were my thoughts almost thirty years ago:

Wisdom: Trusting obedience of God's Word that results in spiritual discernment which is the ability to see life from God's perspective.

Security: The growing awareness of an unconditional personal relationship with the Father that is based solely upon his grace.

Guidance: Faithful pursuit of truth that can only be found as the Holy Spirit reveals the unchanging principles that are contained in God's Word.

Power: The sovereign anointing of God given to yielded individuals that enables them to accomplish supernatural things for his glory.

I would still highly recommend you read *The Seven Habits of Highly Successful People* for both personal and professional leadership development. In my opinion, the best practice book today for creating your Life Plan is *Living Forward* by Michael Hyatt. He delivers on his tag line: "A proven plan to stop drifting and get the life you want."[6]

He provides online assessments and gives you an easy template to follow. I have used this book with many corporate executives, and it has worked extremely well. Read the book and set aside a block of time to be able to hear the Father's voice.

These are the three major categories for my Life Plan:

Personal — Individual Character

Purpose: To maintain spiritual integrity in every area of my life that allows me to experience God's presence, to depend upon his power, and to have faith in his provision.

Scripture: And you shall love the Lord your God with all your heart, with all your soul, with all your mind, and with all your strength. You shall love your neighbor as yourself. (Mark 12:30-31)

Core Value: "Nothing so conclusively proves a man's ability to lead others as what he does from day to day to lead himself." - Thomas Watson

Summary: This part of my Life Plan deals with all the things that relate to me as an individual and are my primary responsibility. I must first learn to lead myself if I am going to be qualified to lead others. In most of these areas, I have the capability to accomplish my goals without help from others, so there is no room for making excuses or casting blame as to why they are not done.

> *You and the Father are in a partnership. He wants you to prioritize your relationship with him and to never try to fill his role in someone else's life.*

Private — Family Ministry

Purpose: To be the spiritual leader in my home and give the best of what I have to offer to the people I care about most.

Scripture: But if any provide not for his own, and especially for those of his own house, he hath denied the faith, and is worse than an infidel. (I Timothy 5:8)

Core Value: I commit to give my family the best of what I have, not just the leftovers.

Summary: This part of my mission statement is exclusively for the ministry that I have for my immediate family members. It starts with the single most important human relationship I have, and that is with my wife. When I maintain oneness spiritually and oneness with my wife, I usually have all that I need to deal with everything else life throws my way. Another important group of people are my children and my wonderful grandchildren. There are many great leaders that can impact the world in the public area of my life, but I am the only husband and father they have and I must do whatever it takes to keep my ministry to them as a priority.

Public — Servant Leadership

Purpose: To be a fully devoted follower of Christ and a servant leader of others.

Scripture: But he who is greatest among you shall be your servant. (Matthew 23:11)

Core Value: It is not acceptable to be an effective leader in one area of your life only to fail in all the others.

Summary: This part of my mission statement deals with all of my responsibilities outside of leading myself and my family. By the very nature of how we live today, this is the area that demands the most time and attention. If we are not disciplined, it will move the most important things to the bottom of the list or off the list completely. Although there are many things in this category that are both good and necessary, we must not allow them to change the definition of a successful life.

PRIORITIES

Now, it's time to start defining your priorities and setting specific measurable goals. I want to show you the latest list of priorities I have in the *Personal* section of my Life Plan. They have changed slightly over the years and I evaluate progress on a monthly basis.

SPIRITUAL RELATIONSHIP

Purpose: To grow in my relationship with Christ and to allow my faith to lead every other area of my life.

Core Value: That I may grow in my relationship with Christ and share my story with others. (Philippians 3:10)

Goals:

Priority Time: Spend a minimum of thirty minutes every morning reading the Word, devotionals, prayer, and personal worship.

Growth Time: Spend two to three hours per week in personal Bible study, watching or listening to messages, and reading Christian books in the evenings.

PHYSICAL FITNESS

Purpose: To maintain a healthy lifestyle so that I can accomplish all the other priorities in my life.

Core Value: Taking care of myself is a fundamental character issue where I have made promises to myself and need to develop the discipline to keep my word.

Goals:

Exercise Program: Maintain a minimum of thirty minutes, four times per week, of high energy walking and strength training in the morning.

Healthy Eating: Minimize fried and fatty foods, add lots of fruits and vegetables, drink plenty of water, watch portion control, and do not eat too fast.

Unplugged Rest: Find a minimum of thirty minutes each day to be alone in a quiet place, preferably outside to unwind and quiet my mind.

FINANCIAL STEWARDSHIP

Purpose: To make a profit so that I can make a difference.

Core Value: I want to increase my income, control my spending, and make wise decisions so that I can provide for my family and help others.

Goals:

Develop Annual Budget: Add additional categories and adjust amounts in each one to reflect financial priorities for the following year by the first of January.

Budget Posting: Post all expenses by category at least once per week on weekends and make any necessary adjustments in spending during the month.

Monthly Evaluation: Print out monthly reports and review if any changes need to be made or any exceptions discussed on weekends.

We all use something like this at work to intentionally track priorities and make sure we are reaching goals. If we value these leadership disciplines at work, why would we not use them with the most important people and priorities in our life?

I simply block an hour time slot at the end of the month and go through an evaluation of every goal. I use a simple rating system:

5: Excellent
4: Successful
3: Satisfactory
2: Needs Improvement
1: Corrective Action

Over the years, I have averaged twenty to thirty specific goals. Based on life change situations, I have to be willing to shift how I spend my time. However, the *Personal* and *Private* priorities have rarely changed because they are the most important and are also more in my circle of influence.

All of my goals are important, so it is rare that I delete any of them. What I watch for are areas that show up in the 1 or 2 evaluation scale for more than a couple of months in a row. Obviously, at times, more things will be demanded at work, and children get sick and need more attention. This is not some legalistic performance system but an honest assessment of how I am spending God's grace.

If I do see a pattern of "needs improvement" or "corrective action" outcomes, then I know I have a resource allocation problem that must be addressed. The demands in our lives change constantly and to maintain our margin, we must either reduce the demands or increase the capacity. For example, I may delay attending a leadership conference until next year because my family needs more of me right now.

On the other hand, I may determine the problem is that I have been wasting daily grace and need to own my capacity problem. I reset my grace account and monitor my daily thoughts and emotions.

This level of leadership intentionality will help to alleviate stress in your life. It will help you identify when to say "no" and when to say "yes." We all live with some level of accountability for priorities and goals in our work environment. Why would we not bring that same degree of proactive leadership to help the people who matter the most?

Your regrets will not primarily come from the outward mistakes you have made but from the relational opportunities you have missed. Francis Chan said it best: "Our greatest fear should not be of failure but of succeeding at things in life that don't really matter."[7]

SPIRITUAL DISCIPLINES

Prayer

I want to share the personal spiritual practices that have proven to be the most important in my relationship with the Father for over fifty years. You cannot be an effective Christian leader without them. If you don't prioritize this, nothing else works. It is the divine equivalent of daily feedback and routine performance reviews. Prayer is an ongoing conversation that only stops when I sleep.

I want to remind you once more of another critical truth: when the Father brings problems into your life through other people, he is wanting to show you something about your relationship with him, not them.

When I completely lose my temper with my wife or children and then apologize to them, I may see it as a sign of spiritual maturity on my part. But if I don't ask for the Father's forgiveness and express my deep sorrow for how my anger offended him, then the relationship has been damaged even more by that omission than through the anger. David's painful confession, "against you and you only, God, have I sinned," must become our prayer as well.

Most of us do well with petition, intercession, and even thanksgiving aspects of prayer, but we fail miserably with the most important parts of confession and worship. Confession is not telling God what he already knows; it is a full acknowledgement of the fact that you now believe the same way he does about your sin.

Most of us wonder every day, "how am I doing?" If you let your emotions or logic answer that question, you will reach the wrong conclusion every time. The only an-

I want to remind you once more of another critical truth: when the Father brings problems into your life through other people, he is wanting to show you something about your relationship with him, not them.

swer that matters is what you believe to be true about God. Trying to process your emotions or make decisions alone is a prescription for failure. Prayer moves you to ask, "what do I believe about God in this situation?" and that is the only answer that will provide the peace that will guard your heart and mind.

It is important for your prayers to be real and raw. God already knows how you feel—if you try to speak to him in King James English, he knows you don't fully trust him.

Another major truth that we must remember is, because of God's indwelling presence, he does everything and goes everywhere with us. So, we should pray about every situation in life:

"Father, please give me wisdom and discernment for how to deal with this difficult one-on-one meeting."

"Lord, help me to see what needs to be done to solve this problem at work."

"God, give me wisdom and discernment to be fully present with every member of my family tonight."

The fellowship here is as deep as anything you have experienced in a worship service. It is where God's greatest desire meets your greatest need and it takes your breath away.

On my way home from work, I developed the discipline to stop and pray for the grace I needed to serve my family. These holy conversations represent the fullest expression in this life of the intimate fellowship between the divine and the redeemed. They are a glorious preview of all that is to come when we will live together forever on the other side of eternity.

Bible Study

Beyond your prayer life, this is the single most important spiritual discipline you will have. As a matter of fact, it is a critical part of your prayer life, as the Holy Spirit uses his Word to speak to you about everything.

Rather than talk about methods and best practices, I want to start by connecting this to three major biblical truths. They come from the familiar stories known as "The Law of the Harvest" and "The Parable of the Soils."

In relationship to Bible study, "The Law of the Harvest" simply means that you will harvest truth in direction proportion to the volume of seeds that you are sowing.

The following Scriptures speak powerfully:

*Man shall not live by bread alone but by every word
that comes from the mouth of God. (Matthew 4:4)*

*Faith comes from hearing, and hearing through
the word of God. (Romans 10:17)*

*I have hidden your word in my heart so that I might
not sin against you. (Psalm 119:11)*

The analogy of eating one big meal a week and then trying to exist on small snacks every morning is spot on. Listening to a sermon on Sunday and watching a video on "Right Now Media" is not going to keep you filled. As you saw in my Life Plan, thirty minutes every morning and up to three hours per week is the minimum for me. However, if you don't learn the lessons from "The Parable of the Soils," none of this effort will produce lasting results.

When we normally hear about or read "The Parable of the Soils" we tend to think the soil is comparing the hearts of Christians and those who are lost. But, in my own life, after reading the Bible through more than thirty times, something was still broken. I was gaining lots of knowledge but almost no intimacy. Martha would be so proud of me, but Mary knew my blind spot.

Today, I read a single chapter over and over again for every truth it has to offer that applies to my life. I circle key words and create my own word clouds so that when I come back, I can quickly be reminded of what I already know.

I often go back to Psalm 139, Ephesians 1, Romans 8, and John 15. This is extremely holy ground to me and never fails to remind me that I live every day securely in the grip of God's grace.

I understood "The Law of the Harvest" but was failing miserably on the major truth of the soils. I finally learned, at least for me, that every time I studied the Bible one of four things would happen—and I had to own the condition of my heart.

If I had no margin in my grace account, I was like the packed down dirt by the road. As soon as I walked out of the building on Sunday, any truth I had heard was already gone. This is why we are often emotionally moved in a worship service but rarely permanently changed.

If I was not maintaining my spiritual oneness with the Father by constant confession, then I had no spiritual capacity to really understand. I would receive the Word with joy but that only lasted for a few days. There were unconfessed "rocks" everywhere in my life and I did not even know it.

The battle for the Christian life is won or lost based on how we personally lead our minds.

If I had allowed the demands and worries of the world, the deceitfulness of riches, and the desire for other things to drain my daily grace account, I didn't experience the fruit of the Spirit in my life. Many times, I experienced the life that thrives on the busyness of the urgent but misses the blessings of the important.

The third major biblical truth that directly impacts the discipline of personal Bible study is this: if you don't use it, you will lose it. This is a nonnegotiable part of the process because, for the Father, your walk always trumps your talk. My advice is to pay far more attention to the condition of your heart than the volume of your study. We have got to move beyond all the performance aspects of worship and, once again, be in complete awe that God has spoken.

It is a dangerous thing as a Christian to sit before the Word of God with no intention of obeying it. The only thing worse is to be so arrogant to think you can live your version of the Christian life without its truths every day.

Strongholds

The Bible tells us that we are made up of three parts—we have a body, soul, and spirit. The soul consists of our mind, will, and emotions. When we are lost and without Christ our spirit is dead, which leaves our emotions and our mind to lead our lives. When we become a Christian, we now have the Spirit living within us, but nothing happens to our body or our soul to immediately change us.

You have heard it many times before that our thoughts drive our attitudes, which eventually produce actions. Those actions, repeated over time, become habits. Those habits will become your character.

The battle for the Christian life is won or lost based on how we personally lead our minds. Our minds are like databases that store tremendous amounts of thoughts, attitudes, and actions over the years.

Our responsibility as Christians is to renew our minds with the truth of God's Word so that we can believe and behave in a way that allows us to live the abundant life.

This passage sums up this responsibility:

> Do not be conformed to this world, but be transformed by the renewal
> of your mind, that by testing you may discern what is the will of God,
> what is good and acceptable and perfect. (Romans 12:2)

According to Ephesians 4, this is a simple three-step process. We put off the old belief and renew our minds with the new belief that leads to the new behavior. What is critical to understand here is that you must first change what you believe before you can change how you consistently behave.

What this means is that you cannot simply stop trying to do the wrong things. You must invest the time to renew your mind with biblical truth so you can believe and behave differently. This is why obedience is critical to spiritual growth.

Here, we see "The Law of the Harvest" at work again: to the degree that you are renewing your mind is the degree you will be changing how you live your life.

Please also remember, it's not just listening to teaching and preaching that brings about this change. You must confess that you have believed the wrong thing about God and then start to live out your new beliefs for them to change your habits and character.

The Holy Spirit works in our souls to convict us when our thoughts, attitudes, and actions are wrong or when our emotions, logic, and behavior are hurting us, our families, and our fellowship with the Father.

Strongholds represent the areas in our lives where the wrong beliefs have led to the wrong behavior for such a long period of time that we are extremely vulnerable to spiritual attack. This passage will become a much-needed truth for Christians living in the 21st century:

> For though we walk in the flesh, we are not waging war
> according to the flesh. For the weapons of our warfare are not
> of the flesh but have divine power to destroy strongholds. We destroy
> arguments and every lofty opinion raised against the knowledge
> of God, and take every thought captive to obey Christ,
> being ready to punish every disobedience,
> when your obedience is complete. (2 Corinthians 10:3-6)

Let's go back to the database illustration to show how this works for us personally. Our minds have the ability to remember all of the painful things that have happened in the past and worry about all the bad things that could happen in the future.

Just because you forgive doesn't mean that you forget the pain. When you do not change what you believe about that pain, then it can come back to defeat you all over again. We destroy arguments or lies that come into our minds by taking every thought captive to obey Christ. We simply reject the lie by replacing it with the truth.

My father said something to me once that was extremely painful. Because I was not a Christian for most of my teenage years, I did a lot of things wrong. I never studied and made very bad grades. Once I began to grow spiritually, even early in college, I began to assume responsibility for my life and, to some degree, had stopped blaming my past. I was working three jobs including one as a nighttime janitor. Time for study was hard to come by other than very late at night. By the grace of God, I began to work hard academically and at the end of my first semester as a sophomore, I made the Dean's list. To put this in perspective, one semester my junior year of high school, I failed every class.

I could not wait to show my father the report. When I arrived at his house, he was sitting down at the kitchen table. To this day, I can still smell what was cooking on the stove. I said, "I thought you might like to see this," and put the Dean's list on the table. He looked at it for a few seconds and threw it back at me where it landed on the floor. "You should have been doing this all along," he said, and looked back down. In that moment, all of the past pain of the previous twenty years came back and it was all I could do to get out of that house.

It took me a long time to forgive him. Even years later, the pain would come back over and over again. This horrible rejection developed into a stronghold. When I was struggling with something else, this whole experience would pop back into my mind.

I kept thinking that I must not have truly forgiven him and that the problem was with me. But, the issue with strongholds is that they represent where the enemy will keep coming back over and over again to see what you truly believe. The truth was, I had forgiven my father. But, because I had not renewed my mind, the enemy would use a new temptation from an old wound to keep me in bondage. So, I would spend time thinking about the event again and the pain would all come back. That would lead to memories of other bad memories, even with other people, and the downward cycle would continue to spiral. Although I had forgiven my father, I needed to ask for forgiveness from my heavenly Father first. *Never forget the process.*

Breaking the power of strongholds requires us to renew our minds with biblical truth so that when we are reminded of that pain, we can bring every thought captive to Christ. If there is no renewal of the mind, there can be no victory over the temptation.

You must accept the responsibility to put all of this truth into your mental database. Our minds in this sense are filled with both truth and lies. Don't obsess over remembering chapter and verse in the Bible, but the truth it holds.

The bad news is that you cannot delete all of the lies, but you can overcome them with the truth. So many times, when we are tempted, the Holy Spirit acts as a search engine looking for truth to combat the lie that we are tempted to believe. If you are fearful or worried, he searches for all the truth you have stored in your mind about faith and trust. If you have not added these truths into your life, the search results will come back, "no matches found."

If you have issues with fear or worry, stop beating yourself up and fill up your database with the promises of God on that particular stronghold. Then, when the temptation comes, the spiritual search engine will pull up the truths that remind you that God has not given you a spirit of fear.

You may have two or three areas where you need to search the Scriptures and memorize ten truths that will set you free from that bondage. Again, don't obsess over the chapter and verse or translations, just remember the truth. When those painful memories from the past or fears about the future come into your mind, the Holy Spirit can remind you of what God has said. That's when your will casts the final vote by choosing to trust the Father by thinking on all the things that are true about him.

I can no longer trust my emotions or reason on any subject more than I trust what I believe about the character of the Father. This process of putting off the lies, renewing your mind with the truth, and putting on the new behavior will last your entire life.

This painful event with my father eventually led me to a deep spiritual truth that I have used for multiple personal temptations throughout my life: you cannot compare what someone has done to you to what Christ has done for you. When the painful thoughts of these moments would come back, I would immediately reject the lie and repeat the truth of God's Word over and over again. Now, even in my weakest moments, the enemy doesn't tempt my mind with that horrible experience in the kitchen. I'm sure the last thing he wants is for me to start quoting Scripture and experiencing that supernatural power in my life. This is when the stronghold is broken.

A stronghold is not something you can pray your way free from with just a couple of prayers. It is all-out warfare, where the enemy will bring his entire arsenal against you. These strongholds can reveal areas in your life of spiritual immaturity where he will either blame you or shame you, depending on your weakest link on any given day. The armor of God was meant to be worn all day, equipping you in your prayer life where the fiercest battles will be won or lost.

The size of your shield of faith and sword of the Spirit, which is the Word of God, is totally dependent upon how much truth you have learned and lived. You will have to fight these battles with the forces of darkness over yourself, your family, other believers, and, most intensely of all, those who are lost without Christ. This is a long way from the consumer Christianity that we see in our culture today.

Paul's words to Timothy are a good reminder to all of us:

> *Share in suffering as a good soldier of Christ Jesus.*
> *No soldier gets entangled in civilian pursuits, since his aim*
> *is to please the one who enlisted him. (2 Timothy 2:3-4)*

I owe the end of my story to both my heavenly Father and my earthly father. After that stronghold was broken, I never wasted any more of my grace account on this painful experience of the past. My bitterness began to turn to compassion as I realized just how hard it must have been to be a single father trying to raise a rebellious son in the 60s.

My father had always said with absolute conviction that he would never live with me. The Father providentially provided several significant change points that gave me opportunities to make grace deposits in his life. The birth of our first child began to melt his hard heart. He developed lung cancer and his doctor was in Birmingham, which was a two-hour drive one way. I was the driver and that's lot of windshield time to get a lot of things said. Due to his failing health, we both eventually sold our houses and built a new one where he could live with us. He did not live much longer, but those last few years became the time we needed for restoration in our relationship.

I now know that God used my earthly father to show me things about my relationship with him, my heavenly Father, that I could not have learned any other way. The most significant of which is that no one, especially me, is beyond the grace of God to radically transform his or her life both now and for all eternity.

DISRUPTIVE TRUTHS

We are all called to be Christian leaders in every area of our lives.

Our personal vision should be to reach our potential for his glory and the good of others.

The Christian life was designed by God to be lived one day at a time.

We have all the grace we need for every daily challenge, but we must not waste it on the pain of the past or fear of the future.

Every Christian needs to develop a Life Plan where they can say "yes" to God's priorities for their life and "no" to everything else.

Work on things you can control and pray about those you cannot and never confuse the two.

The harvest you will reap is more dependent upon the condition of the soil than the volume of the seed.

Learning how to pray the truth you have applied is the only way to overcome temptations and tear down strongholds.

Chapter Eight: Family Ministry

From an application standpoint, this chapter may be one of the most important in the book. It represents our most challenging responsibility of becoming the human expression of the divine reality to those who matter most.

When our relationship with the Father is not our number one priority, our marriages or our children often move to the top of the list. We then put an unrealistic expectation on our spouse or children to be our primary source of security and significance. The inevitable pain happens, and we desperately try to "fix" our spouse or children in an attempt to force them to meet our needs. Eventually, reality sets in, and we end up deeply wounded and hurting the very people the Father gave us to love us the most.

In *The Purpose Driven Life*, Rick Warren says it this way: "The purpose of your life is far greater than your own personal fulfillment, your peace of mind, or even your happiness. It's far greater than your family, your career, or even your wildest dreams and ambitions. If you want to know why you were placed on this planet, you must begin with God. You were made by God and for God and until you understand that, life will never make sense."[1]

We all know that the family in our culture today is in a catastrophic crisis and unless some drastic changes are made, it will cease to exist as we once knew it. The radical far-left agenda combined with a postmodern worldview have totally redefined the meaning and purpose of the family in our nation. Their view now represents the immoral majority in America, and they are relentless in seeking to lead our country and redefine our values. When men, who could be predators, can self-identify as women and walk into a public restroom with children present, then we need to apologize to Sodom and Gomorrah.

Most Christians are either too busy with other things that really do not matter to even care, or they are too defeated by their own family failures to have the moral authority to make any difference.

MARRIAGE

What we desperately need is a clear and thorough understanding of God's plan for the family. Only then can we lead fulfilled and meaningful lives in these very challenging days. I want us to begin by seeing the role of marriage in God's redemptive plan for completing our global mission. It is far more than personal happiness, because God wants it to be Exhibit A for the gospel.

When Christian marriages are failing at basically the same rate as those composed of people who do not know Christ, then we have lost our voice in this culture. That is why we as Christian leaders must do everything we can to help couples fully realize the sacred covenant they have entered into to represent Christ to the world.

Wives, submit to your own husbands, as to the Lord. For the husband is the head of the wife even as Christ is the head of the church, his body, and is himself its Savior. Now as the church submits to Christ, so also wives should submit in everything to their husbands. Husbands, love your wives, as Christ loved the church and gave himself up for her, that he might sanctify her, having cleansed her by the washing of water with the word, so that he might present the church to himself in splendor, without spot or wrinkle or any such thing, that she might be holy and without blemish. In the same way husbands should love their wives as their own bodies. He who loves his wife loves himself. For no one ever hated his own flesh, but nourishes and cherishes it, just as Christ does the church, because we are members of his body. "Therefore a man shall leave his father and mother and hold fast to his wife, and the two shall become one flesh." This mystery is profound, and I am saying that it refers to Christ and the church. However, let each one of you love his wife as himself, and let the wife see that she respects her husband. (Ephesians 5:22-33)

Without trying to debate all that this text says, it is clear to me that husbands are to unconditionally love their wives and that wives in response are to respect them as the spiritual leaders in the home. The marriage is intended to be nothing less than a testimony to Christ's love for the church and our willingness to trust and follow his leadership in our life.

Please understand this is a supernatural dynamic that cannot be successful without total and complete surrender to Christ in every area of your life. If you cannot consistently bring the power of the fruit of the Spirit to this ministry, your marriage will eventually fail.

I owe so much of what I know about marriage to Larry Crabb who wrote, *The Marriage Builder*. He creates a process that supports all of the biblical truth that has already been presented. His first priority is the spiritual oneness that every Christian must have with the Father before they have anything of value to offer their family.[2] It is the equivalent of starting with The Great Commandment before you can accomplish The Great Commission.

Once you have this personal spiritual margin, then you can move on to the next step of emotional oneness with your spouse. When both individuals in a marriage have spiritual oneness, they can then minister to each other and meet their spouse's legitimate emotional needs.

Finally, spiritual and emotional oneness lead to physical oneness where married couples meet each other's need for physical intimacy. If you violate the order of the process, then you are doing nothing more than having sex with another person.

Spiritual oneness understands this powerful truth: we cannot expect other people or other things to meet the needs in our lives that only God can meet. When God is not first, we will try to place our spouse in that position which causes pain for both individuals. Ultimately, we have only ourselves to blame for the pain we experience by forcing our spouse to fill a void they were never designed to fill.

The only relationship that will meet our deepest needs for security and significance without fail is with the Father. His motives are pure, and his methods are effective.

However, we must understand that our role in this grand redemptive plan is to be the human expressions of this divine reality. God would never have commanded me to love my wife unconditionally if I did not have the power to do it.

I have learned over the years that the degree of pain we experience is directly related to the priority we give to something. So, if my wife is having to bear the burden of meeting my deepest needs that only God is able to meet, then her failures can push me into depression. However, if my relationship with God is first, my wife second, followed by my children, and finally my career, then my needs are met in a healthy way to be able to thrive in each of those areas.

For many years, because I was not where I needed to be spiritually, I tried to meet my needs primarily through my marriage, children, and career. All of my priorities were completely flipped, and I was failing. When they failed me, I tried to fix them believing that they were the problem. The end result was that I hurt them deeply, and I began to lose all hope that things would ever get better.

Over time, as all of my efforts continued to fail at an increasingly alarming rate, I had to do something to protect myself from the pain. Crabb nails all of my passive-aggressive behaviors:

- Unwillingness to share deep feelings
- Responding with anger when feelings are hurt
- Changing the subject when the conversation begins to be threatening
- Turning off, clamming up, or other maneuvers designed to avoid rejection or criticism
- Keeping oneself so busy with work, social engagements, entertainment, church activities, or endless chatter that no deep sharing is possible[3]

Spiritual oneness understands this powerful truth: we cannot expect other people or other things to meet the needs in our lives that only God can meet.

He then warns us not to either stuff our emotions on the inside where they can grow like cancer, or go to the other extreme of dumping them on others in anger as payback. I had to find a way to process all of these painful emotions that would help me get back into a ministry mindset.

As I began to grow spiritually, I came to the place of sharing all of my hurt feelings with the Father first in prayer. This is when I learned to be real and raw in my conversations with him. I finally understood that God knew how I felt anyway so any attempt on my part to clean up my words was fake and disrespectful to him. I quickly learned that sharing with him first was a spiritual safe place to process how I was feeling. He would help me move beyond the pain of the moment and bring me back to all of the truth I already knew about him.

God moved me slowly at times from how I *felt emotionally* about a situation to what I actually *thought* about the situation. Then the ultimate big picture perspective: *what did I believe about God in this situation?*

Did God still love me unconditionally regardless of what had happened? Yes

Was his grace sufficient in this situation? Yes

Could he still meet my deepest needs for security and significance? Yes

Was forgiveness still available? Yes

Did he still want me to come home? Yes

When we receive the Father's forgiveness and then extend it to others, an amazing thing happens all over again—we remember that it's all about him, not about us or them.

Psalm 139 flows all over me again in a new and fresh way:

- *He searches for me and there is nowhere he cannot find me.*
- *He knows exactly where I am and what I am thinking.*
- *He lays his hand on me to lead me and hold me.*
- *When I am confused in darkness, he is not.*
- *He formed me in my mother's womb.*
- *I am fearfully and wonderfully made.*
- *My days were written in his book before I existed.*
- *His thoughts about me are more than the sand.*
- *I awake and I am still with him.*

This is worship in its purest and most intimate expression. God refuses to leave me in my sin because he longs for this intimacy. He wants to be the first choice not the last resort.

When we experience these "holy ground" moments, it is easy to adopt the theology that Jesus is all that we need and be tempted to shut ourselves off from those around us. This is not the time to run to another Bible study to hide from the pain of a broken marriage or a rebellious teenager. When you know you are safely held in the grip of his grace then you can risk the rejection of any person over and over again.

The reality is that the Father is now working in you so that he can now work through you to help other people. Though it was painful, he used those who wounded you to teach you things about your relationship with him that you would have learned no other way. Now you should be secure and significant enough to get back into the battle knowing you are going to experience pain. This pain will still show up in your marriage, parenting, and career. However, the pain will only be in proportion to the priority.

All of this is why a fully integrated life is so important in seeing the Father's plan. Family, work, and friends play an important secondary role in giving you some degree of security and significance. That is one of the reasons why we should wake up every day wanting to minister to those we love and have a great day at work. The other reality is that you are also providing a secondary level of grace to them as you help the Father meet their needs.

If you will be willing to put the Father first in your life, and your spouse in his or her rightful place as the single most important human relationship, you can let go of your unrealistic expectations. Then, by God's grace, there is no marriage that cannot be restored and healed.

It is an amazing thing how when faith is first in your life, everything else seems to fall into place. Your spiritual oneness is the fuel that empowers you every day for the Father to be able to work through you. Your faith becomes a relationship to be enjoyed rather than religion to be performed. Your career becomes a ministry platform to impact eternity rather than just a job. Your friends help build you up rather than pull you down. All of your fun is free of conviction and guilt. Finally, your family is no longer a burden to be endured but a blessing to be enjoyed.

With the right priorities, you can be an effective broken vessel that leaks the fragrance of God's grace everywhere you go. Please start with your spouse; they have been hurting as long as you have. Then, give lots of grace away to your children. Let them see daily glimpses of the Father in what you say and how you act toward them. They need hope that their future will be better than the present.

Using human expressions of the divine reality has always been God's plan for our

When you know you are safely held in the grip of his grace then you can risk the rejection of any person over and over again.

role in his redemptive mission. It all starts with your marriage; the world is watching to see what you really believe about the Father.

GUILT/BLAME CYCLE

God's plan for marriage is two people living in spiritual oneness with him and in emotional and physical oneness with each other. If he is not number one, rather than wanting to minister to and meet the needs of our spouse, we will try to manipulate change in them so they can meet ours.

In our own lives as Christians, when we sin, the Holy Spirit convicts us to let us know something is wrong. If we agree with God about that sin, then confession is made, forgiveness is received, and fellowship is restored. If we are not living in spiritual oneness, then we are wired through our fallen nature to try to justify our bad decisions. So, what we do is cast blame so that we can feel better about ourselves and rationalize our behavior in our minds. "Yes, I lost my temper and overreacted, but you should have never said what you did to hurt my feelings." This need to balance out our guilt feelings with blaming others is what allows us to keep our emotional balance.

Remember what I said about our minds storing all that painful data? In the midst of a major guilt-blame cycle, we will bring up things other people did to hurt us that occurred years ago, just to inflict even more pain.

This cycle is more prominent in marriage because we know the truth about our spouse that others never see, and we exploit their weakness. God designed your marriage so that your strengths are meant to cover your spouse's weakness. Two are intended to be better than one.

When you have not properly dealt with your guilt, you will use your strengths to expose your spouse's weakness rather than cover them. You desperately need them to fail to help you feel better about yourself. This is why we keep pushing their buttons when we are in a heated argument. You know the kind – when thirty minutes or two days later you have absolutely no idea what started the whole thing in the first place.

I have seen couples push so hard because they have so much personal guilt, they will do almost anything to see the other person fail. The moment the other person does, the fighting stops, and they walk away. Why? Because, they got what they needed on the "blame" side—for their spouse to lose the moral authority to demand any change from them. That's why you must never try to become the Holy Spirit in another person's life—you are an easy target, but God is not.

If you love your spouse and want to express your gratitude to the Father for his grace, then don't take the bait. There is nothing more potentially powerful with any person in your life than responding with grace when they are desperately provoking you.

Then, they are left with their guilt and nowhere to go for real relief but back to the Father. Fair warning—when you put a loved one in this situation, things may get worse before they get better. They may go to their toxic friends or anyone in a bar who will listen to their sad story, trying to find someone who will agree with them. Eventually, if they are a Christian, the Father will drive all these people out of their life, and they will be left alone in the proverbial pigpen.

Your responsibility during this time is to use every bit of each day's grace to maintain your own spiritual oneness. You must walk in the light to confess to the Father where you had unresolved guilt because you were too busy casting blame as well.

The Father must get all of the "I told you so" temptations out of you and bring you to a full awareness of his restraining grace in your own life. If not for him, you would be the one in the pigpen. You should be begging for mercy for yourself not justice for your spouse. You must avoid becoming the self-righteous older brother in "The Parable of the Prodigal Son" who is not willing to deal with his own pride.

A spiritual discipline that you must develop is, when you catch yourself casting blame, check your guilt account balance. The Father's desire is for you to reach a point of spiritual maturity so that he will be able to work through you more than he needs to work in you.

DEPOSITS/WITHDRAWALS

Just like the guilt/blame cycle, the concept of deposits and withdrawals in relationships has broad applications beyond marriage. As a Christian leader, I am making deposits into my own life on a regular basis to help increase my capacity. In the same way, withdrawals can quickly reduce my capacity and cause me to lose my margin.

When you finish your Life Plan, you will have several life accounts: personal, marriage, parenting, work, and friends, for example. All of these have separate balances that must be maintained to make sure we have what we need to help others. Also, because these relationships are part of the Father's plan to be secondary sources of security and significance for us, that means they are making deposits and withdrawals into our life as well.

The leadership discipline of setting and maintaining realistic daily expectations for these account balances now comes into play. Remember, the pain you experience from a withdrawal is in direct proportion to the priority you have set as an expectation.

The major benefit to a fully integrated life is that you can deal with the ongoing

The Father's desire is for you to reach a point of spiritual maturity so that he will be able to work through you more than he needs to work in you.

changes in these account balances. If I have a major project at work for thirty days, that percentage can increase to meet that demand with no guilt attached. Then, for the next thirty days, I will shift margin back to working out or date nights with my spouse to make more deposits because of that temporary higher work demand. If you are an effective leader at work and that percentage cannot be adjusted back down, then you need another job.

Let's say that 60 percent of your needs for security and significance are coming from your spiritual oneness with the Father. He must be in the primary priority slot and you have to keep making daily deposits to make sure that percentage does not change.

An important concept to understand is that allocation of time does not necessarily directly relate to value or priority. Most of us will spend the majority of our waking hours at work. However, that time allocation can still align to a 10 percent ultimate value. On the other hand, an hour each day committed to spiritual growth can relate to a 60 percent priority or value in your life. The reason we have lost our spiritual margin and calling in life is that we have allowed the amount of time spent to define the priorities in our life. If the Christian life can be fully experienced through the Church Gathered, then we simply check the faith box for the week.

With that said, still up to 40 percent of your emotional needs for security and significance are coming from other people and other priorities. If you have a biblical model of importance, your spouse should be the primary person who makes deposits and withdrawals up to the 20 percent priority, your children 10 percent, and your career 10 percent.

Marriage is the single greatest risk to your margin because it is the most challenging human expression of the divine reality you have. Remember, there is far more at stake here than happiness—it is nothing less than Exhibit A for the gospel to your children and the rest of your relational network.

All of the 40 percent is conditional and therefore involves more risk. People are flawed and will fail you from time to time, and your company may go out of business. Therefore, you must monitor your expectations with a higher level of proactive leadership.

Here is the bottom line: when your spouse makes a deposit into your life, do not, under any circumstances, raise the expectation bar. Why? Because tomorrow they may not have that favorite meal ready for supper, and, if that is what you expected, then you just caused an unnecessary withdrawal. On the other hand, if you have made dinner reservations and your spouse doesn't want to go out because they're exhausted, don't let that become a withdrawal in the relationship account, either.

In working with couples over the years, there is one withdrawal that is the most painful. There will be times in your marriage when you have all of the spiritual margin you need, and your motives are right. You will see your spouse struggling spiritually and will make a sincere attempt to make a deposit. The deposit will be rejected because the spouse is not ready to receive it. You must realize that this is far more about their relationship with God than with you. Remember that everything you are doing is as unto the Lord. Every deposit made on earth in his name will always be deposited in heaven.

I want to end this section by showing you my Life Plan account on marriage. You will immediately notice the differences in the ratio here of fewer specific goals and more desires. Now, you know why.

You may need to have ongoing conversations about how you are doing from your spouse's perspective. What a wonderful opportunity for a one-on-one where many deep deposits can be made.

PRIORITIES — CARING HUSBAND

Purpose: To love sacrificially by giving grace and supporting everything important in her life.

Core Value: My wife is the most important human relationship in my life, and I must prioritize her care and companionship.

Goals/Desires:

Listening: When my wife is talking to me, stop what I am doing to let her know that she has my full attention and that I value her as a person.

Supportive: Make sure the things that are important to her become the things that are important to me, and make sure to put them on my schedule and get them done.

Understanding: Stop reacting and realize she does not want me to fix every problem but to care enough to understand how she feels.

Communication: Set aside time every day to be together and talk. Schedule weekly date nights. Plan trips at least four times per year to get away to rest and relax.

PARENTING

The role of parenting is critically important in our lives. In the church membership covenant, we as parents have already accepted the responsibility that the home is the primary place where discipleship takes place. The good news is that God can

Every deposit made on earth in his name, will always be deposited in heaven.

use other people to be human expressions of his divine reality in our children's lives, too. However, the connection between earthly parents and a child's view of their heavenly Father cannot be overstated.

This parenting role is a divine partnership where we must do our part so that God can do his. We are not only preparing them for a transition to move out of our house, but to move into his.

The bad news is that even if you get it right the majority of the time, there is absolutely no guarantee that your children will trust the Father. If this is you right now, know that God feels your pain as a parent because things did not go so well in the garden with his children, either. Actually, the first scattering that ever occurred was the painful moment when the Father had to cast his children out of his garden that he had prepared for them. No more early morning walks in the cool of the day.

His redemptive mission since that day has been to bring his children back home. There may be no more encouraging words in all the Bible than these:

> And I heard a loud voice from the throne saying,
> "Behold, the dwelling place of God is with man.
> He will dwell with them, and they will be his people,
> and God himself will be with them as their God.
> He will wipe away every tear from their eyes,
> and death shall be no more, neither shall there
> be mourning, nor crying, nor pain anymore, for
> the former things have passed away." (Revelation 21:3-4)

The incredible news is that he has invited and even commanded that we partner with him in this most important of all human endeavors. This is where your calling to be a Christian leader must be prioritized.

You as a parent or even as grandparent must realize just how short your maximum window of influence is over these precious lives that have been entrusted into your care. Their ability to see Christ living in you can help make a difference for eternity.

When I was a parent, we were told what seemed to be an unbelievable truth at the time. Over 85 percent of the people who would come to faith in Christ would do so before the age of twenty-one. In the post-Christian culture that we live in today, that window has been significantly reduced to ages 4-14.

Please remember that the Lord can save anyone at any time of life. Never stop praying for the redemption or restoration of a child in your family.

I always laugh when I see the marbles in the jar illustration used to show the limited time your children have left at home. It is a helpful reminder of the short window of maximum influence during these formative years. However, when you finish this chapter, I hope you realize that your most critical influence may come much later when your children become parents.

Potentially the most powerful word that helps describe our role as parents in partnership with God is "transition." We always need to remember they have the same basic two needs for security and significance that we do. Our role from day one is to be the primary source of that security and significance for them. What we want to do though, with all intentionality, is to slowly transition their dependency from us to the Father.

It should be obvious to all of us that the older a person gets, the more they should be able to understand their purpose in life and assume more personal responsibility for accomplishing it as well. However, we have pointed out that, sadly, many times age has nothing to do with spiritual maturity.

With this assumed natural transition in mind, I want to use six different words to describe all of the different types of roles and relationships that parents should have with their children. Please here me carefully: we never completely stop any of these roles as long as we are parents. However, we must change our priorities over the years if the transition is to be fully successful.

Protection

When a child is very young, they are completely dependent upon their parents to keep them safe from any danger and to meet every need in their life. This is one of the most significant change points in any person's life. Most parents do this well because this is one of the strongest natural drives that a parent can have, and it never completely goes away as long as you live. The other good news for this time is that for the most part the children are receptive to the love you want to give.

Although these first couple of years can be extremely exhausting, they can also be some of the most rewarding. As Christian leaders, you must shift your schedules to provide enough margin, especially to mom, to make sure everyone does not crash. Husbands and wives must communicate so that unrealistic expectations do not develop. Sometimes, Mom just needs a nap and help with the laundry. The recipient, not the giver, always gets to determine the value of all deposits.

Instruction

The second responsibility of a parent also comes pretty naturally. This involves far more than just teaching them the difference between right and wrong. This should be seen as Character Development 101 for all of life. There is a lot we need to tell our children but far more that we need to show them.

I remember one time I turned around and drove back to a McDonald's, not because the order was wrong, but because they had given me too much change. I went inside and waited in line to simply return the money.

My explanation to the person behind the counter in front of my children was that I was a Christian and it was the right thing to do. I am not sure if my actions moved him closer to Christ, but the example my children saw certainly did.

Fortunately, my wife and I were in agreement about lessons that needed to be learned in public. After one clear warning to our children about bad behavior, we have walked out of more than one restaurant without finishing our food to teach our children that we meant business. We could not have cared less about what the people in the restaurant thought. We cared a great deal about the lessons our children learned.

I would also take my children with me when we would give food away to others in need. The visual image of them putting food into empty cabinets and refrigerators cannot be duplicated in a conversation alone.

In our culture today, real life skills are incredibly undervalued. As a parent, you should teach your children to do everything from tying their shoes and riding a bike to doing laundry, cooking, and eventually driving a car.

Correction

This is the area where parenting can become more difficult and, if you are not spiritually mature as a parent, problems will show up. The key to biblical correction is to respond with the right balance of grace and truth based on the problem.

It is also absolutely necessary to make sure the marriage emotional oneness account has a positive balance so you and your spouse can meet these challenges together. Children are masters at finding alignment gaps between mom and dad. They have also earned at an early age that if they can push your buttons to the point you blow it, their punishment will probably be less. It's the whole guilt/blame cycle in reverse.

When I am teaching on parenting, I love to pose the following situation to the group:

Your thirteen-year-old is dropped off at the movies with their friends and are supposed to be going to a G-rated movie. When you press them about it later, you find out they slipped into an R-rated movie instead.

> *The key to biblical correction is to respond with the right balance of grace and truth based on the problem.*

I poll the entire room and ask how many of you think this is a crisis-level problem, a serious-level problem, or minor-level problem. Almost all of the parents of pre-schoolers raise their hands immediately on crisis-level, the parents of first through sixth graders usually see it as a serious problem, and the parents of the teenagers almost all vote only minor-level. The parents in the room who are at the empty nest stage have a smirk on their face and think the illustration is humorous.

While any form of lying is serious, you cannot kick your children out of the house for this specific issue, either.

A spiritually mature Christian leader knows that it is never enough to know the right thing. You have to say the right thing at the right time in the right way or it's wrong.

A thirteen-year-old who just walked into the house after being bullied and failing a major test is not going to be open to hearing about cleaning up their room no matter how messy it is. I am not saying to not bring up the messy room, but this would not be the time.

Jesus always brought the right balance of grace and truth into every conversation. The conversations with the Samaritan woman and the woman caught in adultery are perfect illustrations. He expressed outrageous grace with both, but he also said, "sin no more." We must understand that grace is the most noticed when it is the least deserved.

Back to the illustration of the struggling thirteen-year-old—they walk into the same house, but with none of the normal daily audit questions about their performance. They can't wait to get to the safety of their own room so they can cry it out. When they open the door, they find their room has already been cleaned and all they have to do is enjoy this safe space.

At this point, don't ruin the kind gesture by trying to claim credit for what you did. In reality, all that you did was become the human expression of the divine reality. You have pointed them to the Father by treating them like he treats you.

There are hills worth dying on—just look to the Father and how he relates to us. The prodigal may need to be released, but never change the lock on the door.

Encouragement

For the dependency transition to be complete, you must move through the next three phases. I will also remind you that you never stop any of the phases, including protection, instruction, and correction.

It is so important for us as Christians to use words that help build people up instead of tear them down. This is crucial for parents during the teenage years. If all your thirteen-year-old hears is "do this and don't do that or you'll be grounded for life," they are going to be discouraged and angry. The worst part is they are not going to want to trust the Father either because they will assume he is a worst version of you.

The single most awesome responsibility Christian parents have is to model the Father for our children. If you are legalistic and overly protective, then they are going to believe that he is as well.

By the time a child reaches their pre-teen years, they need to hear more about what they are doing right than all they are doing wrong. Constant instruction and over correction without generous encouragement and grace is a certain prescription for insecurity and rebellion.

You must wake up every day with the goal of finding something your pre-teen is doing well and encourage them about it.

> *Fathers, do not provoke your children,*
> *lest they become discouraged. (Colossians 3:21)*

I still get a lot of pushback on what I am about to say. Based on the extremely toxic culture our teenagers are battling, I would shift the percentage of grace at home to 80 percent and truth to 20 percent during high school. I am sorry, but clean rooms are not even on my top ten list of concerns anymore. Home needs to be a grace zone. Everywhere else in their life is a war zone and people are literally dying.

Coaching

I have found over the years that the next stage of parenting is the biggest hill to climb for most people. We must go beyond encouragement to assume the relationship of a coach.

You know you are entering this stage when your children come to you with stories about what "other people" at school are doing wrong. There should be a warning label on this type of conversation that reads, "this is a test and do not overreact." All they want is to see if you will listen and how you will respond.

Let me tell you something fundamentally important about being a coach. For coaching to work, the coach must always be willing to wait for the person in trouble to be willing to admit there is a problem and want to change.

Instruction and correction are probably not going to be effective at this point. Does that mean you should just give up and let your sixteen-year-old behave however he or she wants? Absolutely not—the Father is still watching.

However, you must understand that if your teenager is doing drugs, their real problem is not the drugs; it is an unsuccessful transition. They are getting their security and significance met through friends and fun and not their faith.

Assuming the role of a coach requires a tremendous amount of spiritual discipline on your part. Coaches have to learn how to listen rather than reacting with condescending quick fixes. Coaches have to learn how to wait on the Father and be patient even while the person you love is failing right in front of your eyes. The Father loves them more than you do and, if they will not change for him, they are certainly not going to change for you.

Even more important is the truth that if you want to be able to fully trust the Father with your children, then you must first be willing to completely trust him with yourself.

For coaching to work, the coach must always be willing to wait for the person in trouble to be willing to admit there is a problem and want to change.

Friendship

The last type of relationship a parent should have with a child is that of a friend. A true friend only wants what is best for you and is willing to do anything to meet your needs. True friendship means there are no more hidden agendas. If I am your friend, it means that I choose you to be an intimate part of my life—not because I have to, but solely based on the fact I want you in my life.

Children do not get to choose their parents and most parents do not get to choose their children. All of us, though, get to choose our friends.

Regardless of all that has failed in the past, forgiveness, redemption, and restoration are still possible. Never stop praying, changing, and taking the risk of being hurt again by reaching out.

Friendships are based solely on love, respect, and trust rather than obligation and mere responsibility. Friends still must step up at times and speak the truth that needs to be heard.

Trust me, when parents and children make it through all of these stages, the most meaningful expression of their relationship is when they both choose to become friends for life. The withdrawals are few and the deposits are many because the spiritual transition to the Father has occurred.

Trust me, when parents and children make it through all of these other stages, the most meaningful expression of their relationship is when they both choose to become friends for life.

PERSONAL FAILURES

This may be the hardest part of this book to write for me. I often wonder if the degree of the pain I experienced as a child caused me to set the bar too high for everyone else in my family. This is not intended to be an excuse for my bad parenting. It is a reminder to all of us to never bring the unresolved pain of our past into the next phase of our life. The people who end up getting hurt the most were not the ones who failed you.

As already mentioned, sometimes parents can do all the right things and children will not make good choices. We, as parents, though, must also own our part of the responsibility when these transitions are unsuccessful.

If you are a parent reading this who does not have faith and your marriage in their rightful place, then your children can easily move to the top of the list. You must get them in the right place, after your relationship with God and your spouse, for their sake and yours.

By the time they enter middle school, their friends have moved to the top of their list. Then college, career, and a spouse of their own with another set of parents to compete with for Christmas holidays. You have now moved from first in their early childhood to maybe fifth or sixth place. What feels like a lack of gratitude by their pulling away is nothing more than their transition into adulthood.

The real problem is that you had placed them way too high for way too long near or on the top of your emotional needs list. This is not a sinful stronghold that needs to break, but a massive blind spot that needs to be resolved. To the degree that this is true, you will fight the transition of releasing your children every time, not because it is not best for your children, but because it is not best for you. This is a very painful admission but a very necessary one if their relationship is going to become all that the Father intended for it to be.

Far too many parents are trying to live out their own fantasies or dreams through their children and that is an unrealistic expectation to put on them. Also, our need to be seen by our peers as a great parent can also bring toxic emotion into our parenting.

The cold hard truth is that when my children would fail, it would make me feel like I failed, too. In reality, the real failure on my part was caring about other people's opinions of me more than what was best for my children. This was such a major failure in my life that I had to seek God to find out why this was a struggle for me. It went all the way back to my own relationship with the Father.

Most of the time we parents tend to forget that we are also children. I used to complain and whine to the Father about why my children kept making the same mistakes over and over again when they knew the difference between right and wrong.

Why were they making the same dumb decisions all the time? Why were they so unwilling to assume responsibility and be under my authority? What hurt more than anything else: why were they so ungrateful after all that we had done for them? Eventually, the Father gave me an answer: "it's the same reason that you do not follow my leadership and are not grateful to me." Finally, it became clear to me that I had expectations of my children as their earthly father that were far greater than my own willingness to respond to my heavenly Father.

Just as the Father wants our children to transition through all six of the phases of parenting relationships with us, he wants us to do the exact same thing with him spiritually. The clear difference, though, is the spiritual parenting transition is never delayed because of poor parenting, but because of a lack of trust and faith on the part of the children in the Father.

If the only way the Father can relate to us is through constant instruction and correction rather than encouragement and friendship, then the total responsibility lies with us not with him.

The bottom line is this: your stage of spiritual maturity as a child will directly be related to your leadership style as a parent. If all you know from your relationship with the Father is instruction and correction with a heavy dose of guilt motivation included, then that is exactly how you are going to parent your children.

Let me wrap up this chapter with the most serious issue of all. I said earlier that your greatest responsibility as a parent was to model the Father for your children. An even greater responsibility as a Christian is to model Jesus Christ to the world—to your friends, co-workers, neighbors, customers, teachers, every person you meet.

You are the only sermon many of them will ever hear. As they listen and watch you every day, what are you teaching them about Jesus? The Christian life is nothing more, or certainly nothing less, than responding to all of the other people in your life in the same way the Father has responded to you.

You can never pass on to other people something you have not first received yourself. The key to parenting and to the Christian life is not about being a great mom or dad, but all about being a grateful son and daughter. When you finally understand that, your life will dramatically change because your focus will no longer primarily be about yourself, but about God and those around you. Welcome once again to Christianity in the 21st century.

The bottom line is this: your stage of spiritual maturity as a child will directly be related to your leadership style as a parent.

The Christian life is nothing more, or certainly nothing less, than responding to all of the other people in your life in the same way the Father has responded to you.

DISRUPTIVE TRUTHS

Marriage is Exhibit A for the gospel to our children and to the world.

As followers of Christ, husbands are to unconditionally love their wives, and wives are to humbly respect their husbands.

When our faith and our family are not our top priorities, nothing else works.

Christian leaders must set and maintain realistic expectations for everything.

Sharing your raw pain with the Father will give you new perspective and gratitude.

When there is no guilt there is no need for blame.

Margin is maintained when the deposits are greater than the withdrawals.

Parenting is a partnership with the Father that results in a successful transition.

You cannot pass on to someone else what you have not first received yourself.

Chapter Nine: Career Calling

Since you are still reading at this point, congratulations on working through the whole process. My prayer has been that something I have written in these pages will move you closer to Christ and to living out his calling for your life.

Throughout this book, I have used two key words to describe all of us, and those words are "Christian leader." Whether you are a church leader or corporate leader or have never considered yourself to be in a leadership position at all, we all share this same calling to Christian leadership.

This chapter is primarily for those corporate leaders who are already committed to merging work and faith. I have already given you several significant reasons why we must leverage this platform for our good and God's glory in the first chapter. This is the area of our public life that demands the most of our time commitment during the week. This means that we have to become the absolute best leaders possible because the demands will always try to exceed the capacity. I will share many best practices in this chapter to help equip you to make sure that does not happen on an ongoing basis. An important truth to keep in mind: as Stephen Covey says, "Just because something is urgent does not mean that it is important."

> *This means that we have to become the absolute best leaders possible because the demands will always try to exceed the capacity.*

We also said in Chapter One that because of divine disruption, work has become one of the most fertile mission fields in the world. As I write this today, one of my friends is doing leadership training in a country that is completely closed to missionaries. Here in America, the three generations that are not going to church are still going to work. Many of their values line up perfectly with current leadership best practices.

CORPORATE SHEPHERDS

When you look at your Life Plan, you will identify certain roles you play in every area of your life. For example, I see myself as a committed disciple in my personal life as the best way to describe my role.

In Chapter Six, I introduced the whole idea of seeing yourself as a church planter. These are not formal church plants, but expressions of Christians working together to accomplish the mission of Christ.

I see my family as the most important expression of the Church Scattered in my life. I serve in the role of spiritual leader in my home, and I want to give my family all of the leadership capability I have to offer.

Neighborhood ministry is another extremely important mission field. This plant of the Church Scattered ministers to widows and intentionally seeks to move lost people closer to Christ.

The last major area of church planting will occur in the marketplace where you work. The expressions of how that will actually take place are incredibly varied, from one-on-one private prayer to company mission projects in the third world.

The best expression of this role for me is the idea of serving as a corporate shepherd. "Corporate" helps define the ministry platform as work. "Shepherd" represents your calling to spiritually care for all the people in this area of your relational network.

In the Church Scattered strategy, corporate shepherds see themselves as Christian leaders who are committed to making a profit so they can then make a difference. They accomplish this by valuing people over process and intentionally seeking the highest return on investment for eternity. They are incredibly aware that their final performance review will be with only one shareholder—the Father. He will want to talk about how wisely they used the resources he allocated, and the metrics that will matter are connected to eternal outcomes. This requires being "all in" on knowing Christ and making him known to those around you. If this is not your level of commitment, then, at the end of your life, all you will have had is a job.

Because you are a corporate shepherd, you can drive business results at a very high level while at the same time seeing opportunities to make spiritual deposits. You have wisdom, discernment, and power that produce the fruit of the Spirit so others can experience his fragrance.

I value all who are called to go to seminary and serve on church staffs or with mission agencies. For such a time as this, the role of corporate shepherds represents the tip of the spear in reaching the world for Christ.

LEADERSHIP DISCIPLINES

Risk Tolerance

We've covered this a great deal throughout the book, but I want to circle back here one more time because, in your workplace, you are going to be leading in a post-Christian, cross-cultural, multi-generational context where spiritual warfare and persecution are present. This goes beyond the disciplines of personal Bible study and prayer, or even having a great marriage and successful parenting. This will require the type of faith relationship with the Father that led Abraham to leave his home to go to an unknown land.

Faith means that I believe that God is able. Trust means that I also believe that he is good. Being a corporate shepherd means that you could lose your job for all the right priorities.

For multitudes of understandable reasons, losing a job is one of the things we fear most, especially as men. I have been without work during four different seasons of my life. The first two were devastating and the third one almost killed me with deep depression. The biblical truth I am about to share prepared me to come out of the fourth transition with faith and hope that something better was about to happen.

Some of this anxiety is clearly driven by getting too much security and significance from work. However, the appropriate biblical priority to provide for our families is a responsibility we should gladly embrace.

When no one will hire you and you have drained all of your retirement, you face the real possibility of losing your house, healthcare, and the ability to pay the basic bills. I promise that if you have to go through this level of pruning, it will force you to tear down every materialistic idol in your life.

> Therefore I tell you, do not be anxious about your life, what you will eat or what you will drink, nor about your body, what you will put on. Is not life more than food, and the body more than clothing? Look at the birds of the air: they neither sow nor reap nor gather into barns, and yet your heavenly Father feeds them. Are you not of more value than they? And which of you by being anxious can add a single hour to his span of life? And why are you anxious about clothing? Consider the lilies of the field, how they grow: they neither toil nor spin, yet I tell you, even Solomon in all his glory was not arrayed like one of these. But if God so clothes the grass of the field, which today is alive and tomorrow is thrown into the oven, will he not much more clothe you, O you of little faith? Therefore do not be anxious, saying, 'What shall we eat?' or 'What shall we drink?' or 'What shall we wear?' For the Gentiles seek after all these things, and your heavenly Father knows that you need them all. But seek first the kingdom of God and his righteousness, and all these things will be added to you. Therefore do not be anxious about tomorrow, for tomorrow will be anxious for itself. Sufficient for the day is its own trouble. (Matthew 6:25-34)

People all over the world know what it is like to be without food, clothing, and shelter. Most Christians living in America cannot even imagine those scenarios and often take these blessings for granted.

The fear of losing your job cannot be greater than your trust in the Father's promise

For such a time as this, the role of corporate shepherds represents the tip of the spear in reaching the world for Christ.

to provide for you. The critical belief from this text is not only does the Father know that we need these things, but we are more valuable to him than anything else. For me, this is the ultimate application of the truth: you will never know Christ is all that you need until he is all that you have. It does not require you to be homeless, but it does require you to be humble.

I have already told you that I have had more divine encounters at work than serving on a church staff. One specifically relates to God's providence in taking care of me. When I was at Reynolds, I was successfully beginning to merge my work and faith. A customer service representative position became available that interested me. Part of the role was to help entertain the company's most valuable clients at a beautiful spot on the lake complete with a large houseboat. Several of my Christian friends advised me not to apply for the job because the environment would be challenging for someone with my Christian values. The problem was, in reading Scripture, I saw that Jesus was always hanging out at parties with lost people.

The risk was that if I applied for the job and didn't get it, it could be a major setback for my career. After lots of prayer, I decided to interview for the position and told the hiring manager that I was a Christian and my personal convictions wouldn't allow me to drink alcohol as part of entertaining clients. When I told my friends what I said in the interview, they all laughed and told me that I had blown any chance of getting the job. Surprisingly, I got the job and, after several months, I was on one of those houseboat rides.

The hiring manager told me later on that my statement about drinking alcohol initially made him angry. Then, the more he thought about it, he decided it might be a good idea to always know that one person on the boat would be sober with all the clients on board. Only the Father can take something that could so easily have been meant for evil and turn it completely around into something good. That was a major deposit into my faith and trust account and gave me confidence for the many more battles ahead.

RELATIONAL NETWORK

When you are a Christian leader and have many different circles of people in your public life, you should include all of them in the same integrated network. They will be in different categories and, therefore, require different levels and frequencies of connection. The same software application will allow you to keep up with your entire network and make sure you don't miss any critical ministry change points.

I think the best way to show you how this works is within my own Life Plan. This set of priorities and goals is specific to my leadership development company. This is a combination of specific goals and prayerful desires.

Priorities — Leading Company

Purpose: To offer a comprehensive platform of leadership development that gives equal value to personal character and professional competency.

Core Value: A great life is not about work-life balance but work-life integration. Balance assumes equal importance and creates win-lose situations. In contrast, the goal of integration is to increase margin, which is the capacity to be successful in every area of your life.

Goals:

1) Content Development

Research: This includes reading, podcasts, webinars, conferences, and meetings, so that I can find relevant best practice materials that would be helpful to others. I spend a minimum of five hours per week in this area.

Writing: This is the first major step in taking this research and my personal life experience and putting it in a format that can be made available to others. Potentially starting blogs and moving to intentional deliverables. This step normally takes up to ten hours per week.

2) Communication Process

Platforms: The next decision is to choose the most effective platform to deliver this material either on a website or in blog, speech, training, coaching, audio or video podcast, social media, webinar, e-book, email, text, or phone call. Converting this content into one of these delivery systems usually takes an hour per day.

Storytelling: This is the intentional communication of all client stories for partners, influencers, active contacts, and to the crowd with the express purpose of getting them to influence others or connect to taking the next step. Time allocation of three hours per week.

Posting: This is where the website and social media seek to provide helpful content and ongoing encouragement. This is a part of staying connected to friends, partners, and active contacts and requires up to five hours per week.

3) Content Delivery

Coaching: This represents the preparation and the one-on-one time I spend with individuals helping them to set priorities and make decisions about what is really important in both their personal and professional lives. This time varies but can take five to ten hours per week.

Training: This includes the preparation and all of the group sessions specifically for presenting content that equips and teaches practical application of leadership principles. Normally the time commitment is one half-day per month.

Speaking: Time spent preparing and presenting inspirational and challenging content to larger groups for the purpose of motivating them to assume responsibility to become a person of excellence and a great leader. Average time commitment is one two-day block per quarter.

ORGANIZATIONAL EFFECTIVENESS

Planning: Time spent planning workflow for the day, week, month, and making ongoing adjustments to schedule. This takes a minimum of four hours per week.

Administration: Time spent sending and responding to emails, scheduling trips, and billing. This takes at least three hours per week.

Evaluation: This is the time I spend evaluating what is working and what is not. It is also the time to dream and think about the vision of what could be done in the future. It must be put on the schedule or it will not happen. My plan is to spend at least two hours per week, half-day once per month, and a full day away from the office once per quarter.

Proposals: The formal submittal of potential services and fees for each client based on their needs and my capacity to deliver excellent results.

BUILDING NETWORK

Purpose: To connect and invest in all the people who are part of my public world.

Core Value: People are not a means to the end in your life, they are the end.

Goals:

Friends (People you feel called to help and will be there for you when you need them.)

Stay Connected: Make sure to maintain ongoing contact with a small group of people who have always been there through the good times and the bad. Try to talk at least once each quarter and plan an in-person visit at least once a year if they live out of immediate area.

Discover New: Always be open to bringing new people into your life that need your friendship and can be an encouragement to you as well.

Accountability: Make sure that you have at least one person in your life outside your family that knows everything about you and can tell you what you need to hear about all of the priorities in your life. Meet with them at least once each quarter.

Partners (All of the clients you serve, the influencers who serve you, and the people you collaborate with to accomplish together what you could not do alone.)

Investing: Staying in contact and investing with existing partner network. Social media and email can help but nothing can take the place of having a meal with someone, meeting face to face, or a phone call. This must remain a major priority, and you need to set a goal of spending up to two hours per week in connecting with this group.

Contacts

Connecting: Intentionally meeting new people through your existing relational network that may need your encouragement, your help, or know someone you need to meet. Moving existing active contacts into partner network. Set a goal of connecting with at least five people in this category per month. This requires a minimum of two hours per week.

Neighbor (Everyone who lives within your neighborhood community and especially those who live very close to your home.)

Connecting: Finding opportunities to meet all your neighbors and hear as much of their story as you possibly can. Take advantage of every opportunity to walk out in the yard and have as many conversations as possible.

Investing: Spending enough time with them to know where they are on the receptivity scale and looking for opportunities to help, especially during change points.

I use the MacBook contacts application to store all of the network activity. I update all of the individual's status and schedule the next time for reaching out weekly. This is critical for effectiveness with everyone from a potential client, neighbor, partners, and friends.

PERSONAL PRODUCTIVITY

Because of the new realities of too many daily inputs without the necessary capacity to accomplish them all, this leadership discipline must move to the top of the list. The ability to say "no" will require the maximum development of both your character and your competency.

For many years, I used the best practice beautiful leather planning systems. The priority here was on efficiency and the ability to get things done. I was prioritizing my schedule but not making sure I was scheduling my priorities.

I love this quote by Peter Drucker: "The effective executives I have seen differ widely in their temperaments and their abilities, in what they do and how they do it, in their personalities, their knowledge, their interests—in fact, in almost everything that distinguishes human beings. All they have in common is the ability to get the right things done."[1]

Technology is worthless if all it does is help you to get the wrong things done faster. However, once you have your Life Plan and a daily system in place to manage inputs, then it can significantly increase your capacity.

The best leadership practice can be found in David Allen's book *Getting Things Done*. (Buy the first edition; rebranding has added in his revised editions too much unnecessary process.) The two power words for his system are "captured" and "discipline." The capture is the organization of all the open inputs and the discipline is only doing what is next.

This is Allen's simple five-step process that I have used for over ten years:

- Collect: Capture all your stuff into one place.
- Process: Separate the things that should be done now.
- Organize: Identify next actions that should be taken.
- Review: Make sure everything is in the right place.
- Do: Work on today's priorities in blocks of time.[2]

I finally grew weary and discouraged every week by transferring all the unfinished things from the previous week into the following week's schedule. I went paperless over five years ago and it has changed my life in an extremely positive way.

When new inputs come in every day, the first step is to delete everything that is not important. If it is important and can be delegated, then that is the next step.

The question should always be, "Could someone else do this as well or even better than I can?" If the answer is "yes," then you must delegate the task, not only to help you, but also to develop others.

If it was not deleted or delegated but is still important, I can choose to delay action to another date. This is when the power of technology is incredible. I use my phone app to capture and schedule all of these important things until later.

If the choice is not to delete, delegate, or delay, then it's time to get to work. By using this process and the same technology, I would estimate at least a 20 percent improvement in my capacity.

Changes in our schedules happen every day and that requires flexibility. The primary reason things don't get done is not because we did not have enough time, but because we did not make it a priority.

EMPOWERMENT

Being a Christian leader requires the supernatural to become a normal part of your life. The conscious awareness of hearing God's voice and seeing his hand should happen to some degree every day.

I began to pray multiple times a day for both discernment and wisdom. Discernment is the supernatural ability to see why something was not working. Wisdom is the insight about what needed to be done to fix it.

In my executive coaching, I am always looking for two things in every leader—the character and the competency to do the job with excellence.

I love helping those who are willing but who are simply unable. Working with those who are clearly able, but who lack character and are not willing is painful.

I want to remind you that all three persons of the Trinity were present in one of the most important leadership meetings of all time. The top line issue was, "How do we move forward with creation knowing it will fail without minimizing either justice or mercy?"

There is nothing on your leadership agenda that the Holy Spirit is not both willing and able to give discernment and wisdom to help you navigate.

For example:

I have prayed for both wisdom and discernment about many meetings that I had to lead.

I have also prayed about hiring and firing decisions.

Discernment is the supernatural ability to see why something was not working. Wisdom is the insight about what needed to be done to fix it.

I have prayed to know if I should walk away from a client.

I have prayed for new vision and the ability to cast it with passion.

I have prayed for operational problems and solutions.

I have prayed for the right words in a difficult one-on-one meeting.

Crisis management became my top competency as a leader, but most people never knew the source of my empowerment.

Once, I was asked by corporate leadership to serve on a team that was trying to secure a contract with one of the largest potential clients in our market. We traveled to their corporate headquarters and participated in many meetings to create an approval process. The first few phases went well, but the first major step was a full day run with our product in their best plant. The plant manager was a superstar within their company. I had hosted him on many houseboat rides and we even ran together in early morning workouts.

He clearly had watched and heard enough of my story that he knew I was a Christian. I had heard a lot about his story with career and family priorities. I watched the trust build and the openness growing.

The big day arrived and there were at least twenty corporate executives from both companies present. There were metallurgists, engineers, corporate leaders, and, of course, sales and marketing.

After about ten minutes of running our material, the back end of the plant shut down with alarms and lots of blinking lights. In five minutes, the whole plant had stopped, and that downtime is very expensive.

Everyone grabbed some samples and went to the lab. It was absolute chaos and I was very grateful that this was not my first rodeo. I walked into the room and looked at two blown aluminum cans. Within five seconds, I saw the problem and within another ten seconds I knew exactly what I needed to do. I calmly walked out of the room, which was only noticed by the plant manager. I went down to the manufacturing floor and showed the line foreman what was wrong. The problem was his and not mine. The plant manager stayed up on the catwalk and kept watching. By the time the corporate crowd came out of the lab ten minutes later, the entire plant was up and running. I never told any of them what really happened.

We all went out to dinner and I told them I needed to slip out early to get some rest. The reality was that I went back to the plant and stayed all night.

As I was leaving around 5 a.m., the plant manager was coming in the building. He greeted me with "Good morning" and commented that they had a great evening. The final review meeting was at 10 a.m. It was shared in that meeting that the plant had set a new production record for the entire company during the test run. The plant manager then said he was ready to skip the rest of the trial as long as I would remain on the account.

If it had been appropriate, I would have stood up with raised hands giving all the glory to the Father. The anointing was beyond anything I had experienced at work up to that point.

I knew this had very little to do with aluminum cans and everything to do with the Father using me to influence this plant manager. When you experience the conscious awareness of God's presence in these moments, it will take your breath away.

According to Scripture, we have the same power that raised Jesus from the dead living within us. Corporate shepherds learn how to do the natural with supernatural power and people notice.

FEEDBACK

Feedback is the leadership priority of having open, transparent, and timely conversations with other people. It is the exact opposite of either stuffing or dumping your emotions on another person.

When leaders are not corporate shepherds, many times they will try to avoid the conflict and simply hope it will go away. Or, show aggressive behavior that uses positional authority and causes everyone to hate coming to work.

There is a high correlation between several critical biblical truths and this corporate best practice. Both require Christian leaders to take the initiative when there is a problem with another person. This represents the character quality that requires us to be responsible for leading ourselves first regardless of how the other person responds.

I like to coach this concept on how to respond as the minority offender. This means that in any relationship problem, when you are not the person primarily responsible, you must own your part first. If your motives are right and you really want to help, then admitting your shortcomings first will give you the best opportunity for a major deposit.

This also lines up with not making excuses or casting blame:

> *Judge not, that you be not judged. For with the judgment*
> *you pronounce you will be judged, and with the measure you use*

it will be measured to you. Why do you see the speck that is in your brother's eye, but do not notice the log that is in your own eye? Or how can you say to your brother, 'Let me take the speck out of your eye,' when there is the log in your own eye? You hypocrite, first take the log out of your own eye, and then you will see clearly to take the speck out of your brother's eye. (Matthew 7:1-5)

It is extremely powerful to say to someone in private or even in front of the whole team when appropriate, I need to apologize for losing my cool in our meeting and I was wrong. Don't expect for them to immediately respond in kind, allow the Holy Spirit time to do his part.

Also remember that even though you may be a minority offender with the other person, you are a majority offender with the Father. Get things right with God first and that will give you the grace you need to give to the majority offender.

There is another major biblical truth that gets abused in corporate culture that can cause the leader to lose all of their credibility and create a toxic work culture. I cannot tell you how many times I have listened to a leader talk negatively about another person to others behind their back. This shows incredible weakness and what the leader does not realize is that they are the ones losing credibility with the team. The reason is simple: everyone listening to this negative criticism knows that one day that could be them.

When you have a problem with another person go to that individual first. This feedback principle lines up with the truth of another critical passage:

If your brother sins against you, go and tell him his fault, between you and him alone. If he listens to you, you have gained your brother. But if he does not listen, take one or two others along with you, that every charge may be established by the evidence of two or three witnesses. (Matthew 18:15-16)

This principle works extremely well in any corporate culture. If you have a team member who is not performing, then you owe the organization that information if they don't respond to your coaching.

True leaders will be proactive and apologize. The next step will be to give clear feedback and provide training and coaching as needed. If the person is responsive, then there may be no need for any more formal communication. On the other hand, you can ask your supervisor or another manager to go with you for the next conversation.

Covey says it best: "To retain those who are present, be loyal to those who are absent."[3]

Passive listening to negative things about other people is assumed agreement. Before I let someone dump on me, I always ask if they've approached the individual first. If not, then I end that conversation.

Once you make the major leadership commitment to give ongoing feedback, then becoming a great listener is the most important skill you will need. In his book *What Got You Here Won't Get You There*, Marshall Goldsmith calls not listening, "the most passive-aggressive form of disrespect for colleagues."[4]

The reason we all do this so poorly with our relationships is that we are listening to respond and not to understand. Part of this is a character problem and some of it is due to a lack of competency as leaders. If our emotional needs are not being primarily met through the Father, then our insecurity will drive us to want to be right. If we have not dealt with our offender status with the Father, then the whole guilt/blame dynamic is fully in play. Sometimes it is as simple as we just don't have the margin to take the time to listen.

You will never be great with feedback if you don't show the other person you value them. Put the phone down, turn off all electronics, or adjust the meeting agenda when someone is trying to communicate with you. Great Christian leaders put this discipline near the top of the list because they want more than anything for others to know they sincerely care about them.

SITUATIONAL LEADERSHIP

This is the corporate leadership skill that aligns perfectly with the ability to discern a person's receptivity axis and choose the best next steps for them. This requires you as a leader to know how to listen well and give great feedback.

In the industrial age of corporate leadership, the followers were responsible for aligning with the leadership style of the leader. Now, with the idea age and the priority of collaboration and empowerment, the leader must know how to align with everyone on their team.

We can see the obvious risk of trying to push too hard with someone who is hostile toward Christ without building trust first. The same issues apply when you are micro-managing someone who is capable of delegation.

Leaders today have to know how to align risk with opportunity, demand with capacity, challenge with skill, and development with competency. This applies to every person or team based on the specific challenge they are facing.

Situational leadership still values direction. When someone is new to the role, the last thing you want to do is to over-delegate.

Leaders today have to know how to align risk with opportunity, demand with capacity, challenge with skill, and development with competency.

I had recently hired a corporate executive to be on our team and wanted him to help lead a major construction project. He had no experience, so we set up weekly meetings to go over a very detailed project plan. This same person, in the same meeting, was asked to lead the development of a focus group to help us make a strategic decision. He had tremendous experience in this area and so all I asked for from him was an executive summary when the project was finished.

In the course of one meeting with the same person, I used highly-directive leadership in one situation and delegated every part of a project in another. This is another corporate shepherd application of the principle involved in using wisdom and discernment. Be prepared to shift your leadership style multiple times a day depending on the person and the situation. The tighter the alignment, the more effective the outcomes will be for everyone involved.

The competencies of situational leadership have strong applications in both personal leadership and family ministry. The ongoing monthly reviews of your Life Plan will let you know how successful you are in every area. This allows you to intentionally shift your resource allocation to create more margin as needed spiritually, physically, and emotionally. Then, your focus as a Christian leader is to live one day at a time by using the grace you have been given.

SPEED OF TRUST

This concept covered by Stephen Covey in his bestselling book *The Speed of Trust* has been a game changer for building healthy corporate culture. There has been a movement for several years to value character over competency in leadership.

I still think character forms the foundations from which all competencies are developed. Initially, qualities like trust were placed in the soft skill category, which means they were needed but could not be measured.

The author raises the importance of trust in every relationship in life. It is, in my words, the result of consistently making more deposits than withdrawals with someone.

Covey says, "While corporate scandals, terrorist threats, office politics, and broken relationships have created low trust on almost every front, I contend that the ability to establish, grow, extend, and restore trust is not only vital to our personal and interpersonal well-being; it is the key leadership competency of the new global economy."[5]

Trust is a function of two things—character and competency. Character includes your integrity, your motives, and your intent with other people. Competence includes your capabilities, your skills, your results, and your track record.

Trust is the full integration of Christian leaders needing to "walk their talk." People know that we really care when we deliver the results we promised. Any gaps between what we say and what we do create trust withdrawals. These withdrawals slow everything down because people are no longer sure they can trust you. The higher your trust account balance, the less you will need to hard sell anything. The application of this in both marriage and parenting are even more important than at work.

I will also remind you that this one thing will also determine your willingness to delegate your entire life to the Father. So, what do you now believe about the character and competency of the Father? Is he really fully qualified to lead your life? Go ahead and apply the same criteria to him because there is no gap between his talk and his walk.

ORGANIZATIONAL CULTURE

This is clearly one of the hottest topics in corporate America today. I have spoken and trained on it several times over the last few years. Simply put, organizational culture is a system of shared assumptions, values, and beliefs, which determines how people behave and work together in organizations.

The absolute best practice on this subject is *The Advantage* written by Patrick Lencioni. He says, "The single greatest advantage any company can achieve is organizational health."[6]

The common values people hold and the way they work together directly impacts the outcomes of every aspect of the organization. "An organization is healthy when it is whole, consistent, and complete, that is, when its management, operations, strategy and culture fit together and make sense."[7]

When leaders are less than honest with each other, then clarity is lost about what is important and what is not. This will result in a lack of alignment and the demands will eventually exceed capacity. The truth can no longer be told because the blame game is in full swing. Leaders are told what they want to hear, and the downward cycle continues. Your best people are hurt the most because they are still trying to drive results while daily cleaning up the mess of poor performers. This toxic culture will produce people who talk negatively about everything because information is now seen as influence.

When I am hired by an organization because their teams are not performing well, I ask to attend their leadership meetings. There is no faster or clearer way to evaluate culture than to watch leaders trying to work together.

The section in *The Advantage* on meeting effectiveness is the absolute best practice material available.[8] I have used the model multiple times with consistent success. The major takeaway is that most meeting cultures include both tactical and strategic items together. This is a major mistake because combining them takes away from the effectiveness of both.

The solution is to have three tactical meetings per month and only one strategic. The tactical meetings should have five to ten items on the agenda and primarily be for problem solving around execution. The strategic meeting is for creative development and major strategic planning. There should be no more than one to two items on the agenda and the meeting should last at least three hours.

The problem with combining the two is that when a great new idea comes up, the normal agenda does not allow for lengthy discussion and that shuts down innovation. On the other extreme, you cannot chase down every idea thrown out in a tactical meeting because you need decisions around these ongoing problems.

I strongly recommend that the final decision maker not be the person who is leading the meeting. That needs to be someone who is skilled at allowing some discussion but knows when to make an assignment to someone for reporting later and move on with the agenda.

Shared project management software should be used, and everyone should be required to keep up with his or her work. Collaboration does not mean that everyone needs to know everything.

Meetings should never be used for people to do their work under the excuse of needing more input. Coordination should be used to make assignments to two or three people to bring back recommendations to the entire team. There are so many meetings today that people don't have the time to actually get their work done. Collaboration is overvalued and should be replaced with more delegation.

Although the meetings are not as formal at home, they are no less important. Every family meal is an opportunity to share common values and listen for gaps in alignment. It is also an opportunity for everyone to be heard and for life stories to be shared. The culture around the kitchen table and during all the car rides sets the tone for everything else. Grace should be freely given and love unconditionally shared.

JUICE IS GONE

There is one final subject that we must cover. The journey toward spiritual maturity is a long and sometimes difficult transition. The change is slow, but the results are incredibly radical.

We are slowly but surely developing the mind of Christ, as we start to see the world as he sees it. We are leaving behind the value system we once prioritized and considered to be the meaning of success. The people and things we looked to for our sense of security and significance in life are either gone or so far down the list that they don't matter as much anymore. (This is the list where all the big houses, nice cars, expensive vacations, and corner offices go to die.)

This passage sums up this transition:

> For this light momentary affliction is preparing for us an eternal weight of glory beyond all comparison, as we look not to the things that are seen but to the things that are unseen. For the things that are seen are transient, but the things that are unseen are eternal. (2 Corinthians 4:17-18)

When we show up for work, and the power, position, pride, and pleasures that money can buy don't own us anymore. Everyone else is so pumped up about the new vision statement or the five-year plan, but no matter how hard we try, we just can't muster up the same excitement. All of the things that used to motivate us no longer have any power in our life. This is when you know the juice is gone.

On some days, this loss of enthusiasm may cause you to feel disloyal to the company and to the team. Now, all you can think about is how you can impact the kingdom, and so you begin to feel confused and unsettled. This is where the old model of the Church Gathered has failed us as Christian leaders. We were told back in the 1980s that if we felt this way, it must be a clear sign that God was calling us to seminary and fulltime ministry. There were no other options available for someone who was absolutely "all in" for kingdom impact.

My prayer is that the priority on the Church Scattered will be the answer for so many to embrace their calling as a Christian in the 21st century.

You can now show up for work every day passionate because everything you do is ultimately for Christ. The power, projects, and position have been fully replaced with the people you are called to impact for eternity. Absolutely make a profit. But then use it to make a difference in the world.

You can drive through your neighborhood on the way home looking for opportunities to make deposits in your relational network. Every five-minute anointed conversation moves a person closer to Christ.

Finally, because your entire life is under the leadership of the Holy Spirit, you have something left for the people who matter most. Baths, bedtime stories, and conversations with your spouse become those sacred moments to be cherished for the rest of your life.

The Church Scattered is now your new wineskin and the new wine is far better than the juice that is gone.

My prayer is that the priority on the Church Scattered will be the answer for so many to embrace their calling as a Christian in the 21st century.

The Church Scattered is now your new wineskin and the new wine is far better than the juice that is gone.

DISRUPTIVE TRUTHS

Christian leaders can plant Church Scattered ministries at work.

Corporate shepherds are great leaders who help meet spiritual needs through work.

The Father has promised to provide all you need, and he can be trusted with everything.

The people at work become part of your relational network to make deposits when ministry is needed.

The reason it was not done was not because you did not have time, but because it was not a priority.

The Father created work, and he wants to help you be successful every day.

Be the first to apologize and listen to understand.

Great leaders learn how to shift their style to meet the needs of others.

Make sure your walk matches your talk so trust can be earned.

Create a culture where the truth can be told and where other people are valued.

When the juice is gone, be sure to put the new wine in a new wineskin.

APPENDIX

Additional Resources

Chapter One: Global Disruption

Books:
The Hole in the Gospel by Richard Sterns
The Frog in the Kettle by George Barna
God Is at Work by Ken Eldred
Good to Great by Jim Collins
Disruption by Mark Deymaz

Organizations:
Business as Mission, businessasmission.com
The C12 Group, C12group.com
Center for Faith and Work, faithandwork.com

Chapter Two: Cultural Disruption

Books:
The Next Christians by Gabe Lyons
The Passion Generation by Grant Skelton
Barna Trends 2018
Understanding Church Growth by Donald A. McGavran

Organizations:
Barna Group, barna.com
Qideas.org

Chapter Three: Church Disruption

Books:
Purpose Driven Church by Rick Warren
The Emerging Church by Dan Kimball
Simple Church by Thom Rainer and Eric Geiger
Transformational Church by Ed Stetzer and Thom Rainer

Organizations:
Thom S. Rainer, thomrainer.com
Orange, thinkorange.com

Chapter Four: Great Omission

Books:
The Pursuit of God by A.W. Tozer
Radical by David Platt
Crazy Love by Francis Chan

Organizations:
Radical, radical.net
Crazy Love Ministries, crazylove.org

Chapter Five: Church Gathered

Books:
The Leadership Challenge by Kouzes & Posner
The Advantage by Patrick Lencioni
Lasting Impact: 7 Powerful Conversations That Will Help Your Church Grow by Carey Nieuwhof
Predictable Success: Getting Your Organizations on the Growth Track and Keeping It There by Les McKeown
Move by Greg L. Harkins
Breaking the Missional Code by Ed Stetzer and David Putman
Lead Small by Reggie Joiner
No Silver Bullets: Five Small Shifts that will Transform Your Ministry by Daniel Im
Transformational Groups by Ed Stetzer and Eric Geiger
Creating Community: Five Keys to Building a Small Group Culture by Andy Stanley and Bill Willits

Organizations:
Reveal, revealforchurch.com
Acts 29, Acts29.com
International Mission Board, IMB.org
North American Mission Board, NAMB.net

Chapter Six: Church Scattered

Books:
You Found Me by Ed Stetzer
About My Fathers Business by Regi Campbell
Conversational Evangelism by David Geisler
The School of Evangelism by Ray Comfort

Evangelism Explosion by D. James Kennedy

Organizations:
Church Scattered, churchscattered.com

Chapter Seven: Personal Leadership

Books:
Beautiful Outlaw by John Eldredge
Enemies of the Heart by Andy Stanley
Living Forward by Michael Hyatt
The Seven Habits of Highly Effective People by Stephen R. Covey
Margin by Richard A. Swenson
The Purpose Driven Life by Rick Warren

Organizations:
Michael Hyatt, michaelhyatt.com
Franklin Covey, franklincovey.com

Chapter Eight: Family Ministry

Books:
The Marriage Builder by Larry Crabb
The Five Love Languages by Gary Chapman
Love and Respect by Dr. Emerson Eggerichs
Grace Based Parenting by Dr. Tim Kimmel
Parenting Beyond Your Capacity by Reggie Joiner

Organizations:
Orange, thinkorange.com

Chapter Nine: Career Calling

Books:
Five Dysfunctions of a Team by Patrick Lencioni
What Got You Here Won't Get You There by Marshall Goldsmith
Multipliers by Liz Wiseman
Getting Things Done by David Allen
The Ideal Team Player by Patrick Lencioni

NOTES

Introduction

1.) BrainyQuote. "Thomas J. Watson Quotes." Jan. 1, 2019. https://www.brainyquote.com/authors/thomas-j-watson-quotes.

2.) Chan, Francis. *Crazy Love: Overwhelmed by a Relentless God*. 93. Colorado Springs: David C. Cook, 2008.

Chapter One: Global Disruption

1.) Sterns, Richard. *The Hole in Our Gospel: What Does God Expect of Us? The Answer That Changed My Life and Might Just Change the World*. 239. Nashville: Thomas Nelson, 2009.

2.) Platt, David. Radical: *Taking Back Your Faith from the American Dream*. 109. Colorado Springs: Multnomah, 2010.

3.) Barna, George. *The Frog in the Kettle*. 29. Ventura: Regal Books, 1990.

4.) Barna, George. *The Frog in the Kettle*. 29. Ventura: Regal Books, 1990.

5.) DeYmaz, Mark. *Disruption: Repurposing the Church to Redeem the Community*. Introduction xxix. Nashville: Thomas Nelson, 2017.

6.) Collins, Jim. *Good To Great: Why Some Companies Make the Leap and Others Don't*. 1. New York: Harper Collins, 2001.

7.) Wikiquote. "Eric Shinseki." Last modified May 14, 2019. https://en.wikiquote.org/wiki/Eric_Shinseki.

8.) Collins, Jim. *Good To Great: Why Some Companies Make the Leap and Others Don't*. 54. New York: Harper Collins, 2001.

9.) Collins, Jim. *Good To Great: Why Some Companies Make the Leap and Others Don't*. 50. New York: Harper Collins, 2001.

10.) Eldred, Ken. *God Is at Work: Transforming People and Nations Through Business*. 46. Montrose: Manna Ventures, 2009.

11.)Goodreads. "J.D. Greear Quotes." Jan. 1, 2019. https://www.goodreads.com/author/quotes/3400717.J_D_Greear.

12.) Eldred, Ken. *God Is at Work: Transforming People and Nations Through Business*. 297. Montrose: Manna Ventures, 2009.

13.) "The World Needs Men Who Cannot Be Bought." Grace Quotes. Published April 3, 2015. https://gracequotes.org/quote/the-world-needs-men-who-cannot-be-bought-whose-wo/.

Chapter Two: Cultural Disruption

1.) Skelton, Grant. *The Passion Generation: The Seemingly Reckless, Definitely Disruptive, But Far From Hopeless Millennials*. 82. Grand Rapids: Zondervan, 2018.

2.) Lyons, Gabe. *The Next Christians: Seven Ways You Can Live the Gospel and Restore the World*. 48. New York: Doubleday, 2010.

3.) Lyons, Gabe. *The Next Christians: Seven Ways You Can Live the Gospel and Restore the World*. 4. New York: Doubleday, 2010.

4.) Skelton, Grant. *The Passion Generation: The Seemingly Reckless, Definitely Disruptive, But Far From Hopeless Millennials*. 82. Grand Rapids: Zondervan, 2018.

5.) Lyons, Gabe. *The Next Christians: Seven Ways You Can Live the Gospel and Restore the World*. 23. New York: Doubleday, 2010.

6.) Kimball, Dan. *The Emerging Church: Vintage Christianity for New Generations*. 49. Grand Rapids: Zondervan, 2003

7.) Barna, George. *Barna Trends 2017: What's New and What's Next at the Intersection of Faith and Culture*. 7. Grand Rapids: Baker Books, 2017.

8.) Lyons, Gabe. *The Next Christians: Seven Ways You Can Live the Gospel and Restore the World*. 8. New York: Doubleday, 2010.

9.) Quote Investigator. "Some People Are Troubled by the Things in the Bible They Can't Understand. The Things That Trouble Me Are the Things I Can Understand." Published September 22, 2017. https://quoteinvestigator.com/2017/09/22/bible/.

10.) Skelton, Grant. *The Passion Generation: The Seemingly Reckless, Definite-*

ly Disruptive, But Far From Hopeless Millennials. 82. Grand Rapids: Zondervan, 2018.

11.) Kimball, Dan. The Emerging Church: Vintage Christianity for New Generations. 67. Grand Rapids: Zondervan, 2003.

12.) Barna, George. Barna Trends 2017: What's New and What's Next at the Intersection of Faith and Culture. 168. Grand Rapids: Baker Books, 2017.

13.) Barna, George. Barna Trends 2017: What's New and What's Next at the Intersection of Faith and Culture. 13. Grand Rapids: Baker Books, 2017.

14.) Skelton, Grant. The Passion Generation: The Seemingly Reckless, Definitely Disruptive, But Far From Hopeless Millennials. 82. Grand Rapids: Zondervan, 2018.

15.) Lyons, Gabe. The Next Christians: Seven Ways You Can Live the Gospel and Restore the World. 39. New York: Doubleday, 2010.

16.) Skelton, Grant. The Passion Generation: The Seemingly Reckless, Definitely Disruptive, But Far From Hopeless Millennials. 30. Grand Rapids: Zondervan, 2018.

17.) Skelton, Grant. The Passion Generation: The Seemingly Reckless, Definitely Disruptive, But Far From Hopeless Millennials. 31. Grand Rapids: Zondervan, 2018.

18.) Hoekstra, Harvey. Your Church and Church Growth. 14. Pasadena, CA: Charles E. Fuller Institute, 1982.

19.) Platt, David. Radical: Taking Back Your Faith from the American Dream. 50. Colorado Springs: Multnomah, 2010.

Chapter Three: Church Disruption

1.) DeYmaz, Mark. Disruption: Repurposing the Church to Redeem the Community. 12. Nashville: Thomas Nelson, 2017.

2.) DeYmaz, Mark. Disruption: Repurposing the Church to Redeem the Community. 15. Nashville: Thomas Nelson, 2017.

3.) Stetzer, Ed. "Revitalizing Church Through an Outward Focus." EdStetzer.com. June 25, 2018. https://edstetzer.com/2018/06/revitalizing-church-through-an-outward-focus/.

4.) Donald McGavran quote: Fuller Seminary, *Your Church and Church Growth* (Pasadena, CA: Charles E. Fuller Institute, 1982), 146.

5.) Warren, Rick. *The Purpose Driven Church: Every Church Is Big in God's Eyes.* 17. Grand Rapids: Zondervan, 1995.

6.) Warren, Rick. *The Purpose Driven Church: Every Church Is Big in God's Eyes.* 32. Grand Rapids: Zondervan, 1995.

7.) Warren, Rick. *The Purpose Driven Church: Every Church Is Big in God's Eyes.* 39. Grand Rapids: Zondervan, 1995.

8.) Warren, Rick. *The Purpose Driven Church: Every Church Is Big in God's Eyes.* 61. Grand Rapids: Zondervan, 1995.

9.) Warren, Rick. *The Purpose Driven Church: Every Church Is Big in God's Eyes*. 65. Grand Rapids: Zondervan, 1995.

10.) Warren, Rick. *The Purpose Driven Church: Every Church Is Big in God's Eyes.* 109. Grand Rapids: Zondervan, 1995.

11.) Kimball, Dan. *The Emerging Church: Vintage Christianity for New Generations*. 69. Grand Rapids: Zondervan, 2003.

12.) Kimball, Dan. *The Emerging Church: Vintage Christianity for New Generations*. 95. Grand Rapids: Zondervan, 2003.

13.) Kimball, Dan. *The Emerging Church: Vintage Christianity for New Generations.* 89. Grand Rapids: Zondervan, 2003.

14.) Rainer, Thom and Eric Geiger. *Simple Church: Returning to God's Process for Making Disciples*. 76. Nashville: Broadman & Holman, 2006.

15.) Rainer, Thom and Eric Geiger. *Simple Church: Returning to God's Process for Making Disciples*. Acknowledgements ix. Nashville: Broadman & Holman, 2006.

16.) Rainer, Thom and Eric Geiger. S*imple Church: Returning to God's Process for Making Disciples*. 26. Nashville: Broadman & Holman, 2006.

17.) Rainer, Thom and Eric Geiger. *Simple Church: Returning to God's Process for Making Disciples*. 68. Nashville: Broadman & Holman, 2006.

18.) Rainer, Thom and Eric Geiger. *Simple Church: Returning to God's Process for Making Disciples*. 62. Nashville: Broadman & Holman, 2006.

19.) Stetzer, Ed and Thom Rainer. *Transformational Church: Creating a New Scorecard for Congregations*. Introduction. Nashville: Broadman & Holman, 2010.

20.) Stetzer, Ed and Thom Rainer. *Transformational Church: Creating a New Scorecard for Congregations*. 7. Nashville: Broadman & Holman, 2010.

21.) Stetzer, Ed and Thom Rainer. *Transformational Church: Creating a New Scorecard for Congregations*. 10. Nashville: Broadman & Holman, 2010.

22.) Goodreads. "Dietrich Bonhoeffer Quotes." Jan. 1, 2019. https://www.goodreads.com/quotes/978699-your-life-as-a-christian-should-make-non-believers-question.

23.) Stetzer, Ed and Thom Rainer. *Transformational Church: Creating a New Scorecard for Congregations.* 26. Nashville: Broadman & Holman, 2010.

24.) Stetzer, Ed and Thom Rainer. *Transformational Church: Creating a New Scorecard for Congregations*. 26. Nashville: Broadman & Holman, 2010.

Chapter Four: Great Omission

1.) Tozer, A.W. The Pursuit Of God. 28. Harrisburg: Christian Publications, 1982.

2.) BrainyQuote. "C.S. Lewis Quotes." Jan. 1, 2019. ttps://www.brainyquote.com/quotes/c_s_lewis_164517.

3.) Chan, Francis. *Crazy Love: Overwhelmed by a Relentless God*. 72. Colorado Springs: David C. Cook, 2008.

4.) Chan, Francis. *Crazy Love: Overwhelmed by a Relentless God*. 26. Colorado Springs: David C. Cook, 2008.

5.) Tozer, A.W. *The Pursuit Of God.* 37. Harrisburg: Christian Publications, 1982.

6.) Tozer, A.W. *The Pursuit Of God*. 38. Harrisburg: Christian Publications, 1982.

7.) Tozer, A.W. *The Pursuit Of God*. 17. Harrisburg: Christian Publications, 1982.

8.) Tozer, A.W. *The Pursuit Of God*. 96. Harrisburg: Christian Publications, 1982.

9.) Tozer, A.W. *The Pursuit Of God*. 31. Harrisburg: Christian Publications, 1982.

10.) The Ranch. "Corrie ten Boom—Every experience God give us..." January 29, 2009. https://theranch.org/2009/01/29/corrie-ten-boom-every-experience-god-give-us/.

11.) Sterns, Richard. *The Hole in Our Gospel: What Does God Expect of Us? The Answer That Changed My Life and Might Just Change the World*. 3. Nashville: Thomas Nelson, 2009.

12.) Chan, Francis. *Crazy Love: Overwhelmed by a Relentless God*. 145. Colorado Springs: David C. Cook, 2008.

13.) Platt, David. *Radical: Taking Back Your Faith from the American Dream*. 19. Colorado Springs: Multnomah, 2010.

Chapter Five: Church Gathered

1.) Platt, David. *Radical: Taking Back Your Faith from the American Dream*. 73. Colorado Springs: Multnomah, 2010.

2.) Lyons, Gabe. *The Next Christians: Seven Ways You Can Live the Gospel and Restore the World*. 120. New York: Doubleday, 2010.

3.) Hawkins, Greg and Cally Parkinson. *Move*. 22. Grand Rapids, MI: Zondervan, 2011.

4.) Rainer, Thom and Eric Geiger. *Simple Church: Returning to God's Process for Making Disciples*. Acknowledgements. Nashville: Broadman & Holman, 2006.

5.) The Village Church Institute. "About the Institute." Jan. 1, 2019. https://institute.thevillagechurch.net/institute-about.

6.) Goodreads. "Mother Teresa Quotes." Jan. 1, 2019. https://www.goodreads.com/quotes/106242-if-you-can-t-feed-a-hundred-people-feed-just-one.

Chapter Six: Church Scattered

1.) Stetzer, Ed and Thom Rainer. *Transformational Church: Creating a New Scorecard for Congregations*. 78. Nashville: Broadman & Holman, 2010.

2.) Stetzer, Ed and Thom Rainer. *Transformational Church: Creating a New Scorecard for Congregations*. 83. Nashville: Broadman & Holman, 2010.

3.)Stetzer, Ed and David Putman. *Breaking the Missional Code: Your Church Can Become a Missionary in Your Community*. 48. Nashville: Broadman & Holman, 2006.

4.) Kimball, Dan. *The Emerging Church: Vintage Christianity for New Generations*. 95. Grand Rapids: Zondervan, 2003.

5.) Tyson Foods. "Home Page." Jan. 1, 2019. https://www.tysonfoods.com.

6.) Hobby Lobby. "Home page." Jan. 1, 2019. https://www.hobbylobby.com.

7.) Barnhart Crane. "Home Page." Jan. 1, 2019. https://www.barnhartcrane.com.

8.) Highland Harvesters. "Home Page." Jan. 1, 2019 https://www.highlandharvesters.com.

Chapter Seven: Personal Leadership

1.) Brainy Quote. "Thomas J. Watson Quotes" Jan. 1, 2019 https://www.brainyquote.com/authors/thomas-j-watson-quotes.

2.) AZ Quotes. "The tragedy of life is not that it ends so soon, but that we begin it so late." Jan. 1, 2019 https://www.azquotes.com/quote/531481.

3.)Goodreads. "Phillips Brooks Quotes." Jan. 1, 2019 https://www.goodreads.com/quotes/301052-dreadful-will-be-the-day-when-the-world-becomes-contented.

4.) Covey, Stephen R. *The 7 Habits of Highly Effective People: Powerful Lessons in Personal Change.* 109. New York: Simon and Shuster, 1989.

5.) Goodreads. "Francis Chan Quotes." Jan. 1, 2019 https://www.goodreads.com/quotes/249877-our-greatest-fear-should-not-be-of-failure-but-of.

Chapter Eight: Family Ministry

1.) Warren, Rick. *The Purpose Driven Life: What on Earth Am I Here For?* 21. Grand Rapids: Zondervan, 2012.

2.) Crabb, Larry. *The Marriage Builder*. 29. Grand Rapids: Zondervan, 1992.

3.) Crabb, Larry. *The Marriage Builder*. 33. Grand Rapids: Zondervan, 1992.

Chapter Nine: Career Calling

1.) Goodreads. "Peter F. Drucker Quotes." Jan. 1, 2019 https://www.goodreads.com/author/quotes/12008.Peter_F_Drucker.

2.) Allen, David. *Getting Things Done: The Art of Stress-Free Productivity*. 24. New York: Penguin Group, 2001.

3.) Goodreads. "Stephen R. Covey Quotes." Jan. 1, 2019 https://www.goodreads.com/quotes/76435-to-retain-those-who-are-present-be-loyal-to-those.

4.) Goldsmith, Marshall. *What Got You Here Won't Get You There: How Successful People Become Even More Successful*. 40. New York: Hyperion, 2007.

5.) Covey, Stephen M. R. *The Speed of Trust: The One Thing that Changes Everything*. 26. New York: Free Press, 2006.

6.) Lencioni, Patrick. *The Advantage: Why Organizational Health Trumps Everything Else in Business.* 1. San Francisco: Jossey-Bass, 2012.

7.) Lencioni, Patrick. *The Advantage: Why Organizational Health Trumps Everything Else in Business*. 19. San Francisco: Jossey-Bass, 2012.

8.) Lencioni, Patrick. *The Advantage: Why Organizational Health Trumps Everything Else in Business*. 17. San Francisco: Jossey-Bass, 2012.